ALDSW

The History   village

JESSICA STAWELL

with drawings by Richard Harrow

New Clarion Press

© Jessica Stawell 2002

The right of Jessica Stawell to be identified as the author of this work has been asserted in accordance with the Copyright, Designs and Patents Act 1988.

First published 2002

New Clarion Press
5 Church Row, Gretton
Cheltenham GL54 5HG
England

New Clarion Press is a workers' co-operative.

All rights reserved. Except for the quotation of short passages for the purposes of criticism and review, no part of this publication may be reproduced, stored in a retrieval system or transmitted, in any form or by any means, electronic, mechanical, photocopying, recording or otherwise, without the prior consent of the publisher.

This book is sold subject to the condition that it shall not, by way of trade or otherwise, be lent, resold, hired out or otherwise circulated without the publisher's prior consent in any form of binding or cover other than that in which it is published and without a similar condition including this condition being imposed on the subsequent purchaser.

A catalogue record for this book is available from the British Library.

ISBN paperback   1 873797 39 7
      hardback   1 873797 40 0

Cover photos: lambs from the Aldsworth flock of Cotswold sheep;
               shepherd Jim Wilcox with Cotswold sheep
               © the Garne family

Designed and typeset in Palatino by Rebecca Wilby
Printed in Great Britain by MFP Design and Print, Manchester

This book is dedicated to all the good people in Aldsworth who gave us such a warm welcome when we first came here in 1978.

CONTENTS

PLATES

1. Detail of Aldsworth Enclosure Map, 1799. D 1388 Box C.
    © Gloucestershire County Record Office.
2. John 'Crump' Dutton, 1594–1657. Attributed to Franz
    Cleyn. © The National Trust/John Hammond.
3. Sir Ralph Dutton, Bt, 1642/3–1721. Painting by Samuel
    Browne. © The National Trust/John Hammond.
4. Sir John Dutton, Bt, 1682–1743. Manner of Enoch Seeman.
    © The National Trust/John Hammond.
5. James Lenox Naper Dutton, 1712–1776. Attributed to
    George Knapton. © The National Trust/John Hammond.
6. The Bibury Club Welter Stakes, run on the Old Course,
    16 June 1801. Painted by Henry Bernard Chalon and
    engraved by Charles Turner, 1802. © Major R. W. Naesmyth
    of Posso.
7. View from Aldsworth Church (looking north): 'The
    Barracks', Wall Farm (distance), Pear Tree Cottages
    (centre).
8. Gravestones in the churchyard: John Waine, 1738–76, and
    his wife, Mary Waine.
9. Gravestones in the churchyard: Richard Waine, 1765–1821,
    and his wife, Lucy Waine, 1765–1839.
10. The former school, 2001.
11. The Old School House, 2001.
12. Green Farm House, 2001.
13. Howard's Barn, now Windrush House, 2001.
14. View of Green Farm from the main Cirencester–Burford
    road, 2001.
15. Howard's Cottage, 2001.
16. Detail of Aldsworth Enclosure Map, 1799. D 1388 Box C.
    © Gloucestershire County Record Office.

Plates 7–15 © Jessica Stawell.

ACKNOWLEDGEMENTS

I would like to thank the inhabitants of Aldsworth past and present for contributing information. A list is given in Appendix E. In particular I would like to thank Ken Taylor for his encouragement and for setting up some interviews; and I thank Ted A'bear, Sue Garne, the late Maurice Willes, Ken Stevens and Frank Simpson for consenting to be interviewed.

The late Gregory Phillips, knowing that I was interested in history, kindly gave me a copy of his mother's brief life of his father, for which I am grateful.

The contribution made by David M. Waine to this work has been enormous. He supplied a wealth of information about the Waine family, without which it would have been impossible for me to write the book (see Appendix E). He also very generously provided full print-outs of censuses of population for 1851, 1861, 1871 and 1891, and helped with the preparation of some parts of the book.

I would like to thank Major R. W. Naesmyth of Posso for advice on military matters; for photocopies of parts of the 1800 Army List; and for the photograph of a print of a scene at the racecourse in 1801.

I would also like to thank Judith Curthoys, the Archivist at Christ Church, Oxford, for her help, Ken Taylor for Appendix D, and Raymond and Joan Moody for information and advice.

Samantha Hope typed the manuscript with professional skill and efficiency for which I am grateful.

Finally I would like to thank my husband for his patience and tolerance and for the use of his library.

PREFACE

The original aim of this work was to provide a history of
their village for the people of Aldsworth. However, as the
work proceeded it started to be written for its own sake. As a
result it should be of value to all who are interested in the
history of the Cotswold area; although, of course, it will be of
most interest to the inhabitants of Aldsworth past and
present and their descendants.

In Part I an attempt has been made to write a continuous
and comprehensive history covering the last thousand years,
linking throughout what was happening in the village with
events in the wider world. For the first 500 years this history
has had to be written in fairly general terms. Few of the
records of the great monasteries, which controlled Aldsworth
then, have survived and almost nothing is known of the
people who actually lived in the village. For the following
two centuries there is much more information, but again most
of it is about general events in the area, and about wealthy
and powerful individuals who did not actually live in the
parish, such as members of the Dutton family of Sherborne.
Most of this has been included, for it was these events and
these people who influenced life in the village. No cache of
personal or business papers, letters or diaries relating to
Aldsworth has come to light for this period – or indeed for
any other period. Perhaps this is not surprising for a village
with only a few hundred inhabitants?

For the eighteenth and early nineteenth centuries use was
made of the paper on the racecourse by this author, published
in 1980 and, in a revised version, in 2000. The official records
of racing and contemporary books and articles were used to
write this. Papers of the Dutton family in Sherborne for this
period would have been very useful – had they existed. Most
of the family's papers were lost or destroyed in about 1830.

Fortunately, for the eighteenth and nineteenth centuries
there was also a mass of information collected from the
public records and from many other sources by a descendant
of one of the most colourful characters known to have lived
in the village. A great deal of detective work has gone into

combining this treasure trove with information from other sources, to build up a picture of some of the influential people living in the village at that time. This has been very rewarding to do, because up to now almost nothing has been known about these individuals. Information from the Enclosure Act of 1793 and, more especially, from the Enclosure Map of 1799 helped here.

For the nineteenth century the excellent book on the Garne family published in 1984 provided much information. In addition, a lucky chance find in the library of Christ Church, Oxford, illuminated some important events that took place in the middle of the century. The ten-year censuses of population provided many facts. The 1841 census was the first to give names, ages and occupations of the inhabitants of each household; and that census, and those which followed every ten years until 1891 (the last currently available to the general public), provided a great deal of information.

For the twentieth century a useful source has been the reminiscences and eyewitness reports of people still living in or near the village. As many as possible of these precious memories have been included.

Part II of the book deals separately with the various houses, farms and areas of the village. It will be of most interest to people living in the village or those with a special interest in one building or area.

Finally there are appendices, maps and pictures.

INTRODUCTION

A LDSWORTH is a village with a population of about 200 in the east of the county of Gloucestershire. A glance at a map shows that it is relatively isolated. The nearest neighbouring villages to the north, south and west, Sherborne, Coln St Aldwyns and Bibury, are 3–4 miles away. This gives the village a strong sense of identity. The small town of Burford is 6 miles to the east and the town of Cirencester 10 miles to the south-west. Northleach is 4 miles to the north-west.

Unlike most Cotswold villages, Aldsworth is not on or near a river. Instead settlement developed round a series of springs running north to south. The River Leach forms the western boundary of the parish, but it is a small river running underground for much of its course, as its name implies.

The parish covers an area of 3,350 acres. The land is on the Great Oolite rock, which was laid down as the bed of a shallow tropical sea millions of years ago and is full of tiny fossils. It is overlaid with the less permeable Forest Marble on the high ground to the south-east and west, and is on average 150 metres above sea level. There is very little woodland, and it always seems to be windy. The soil is stony and not very fertile, but it is well drained and suitable for sheep farming. The buildings in the parish and the walls round the fields are made of the local stone, as is usual in the Cotswolds. In this area it is light grey in colour.

Throughout the village's history farming has been the main economic activity, and for most of the time the only one. The type of farming that prevailed was what was and is described by local farmers as 'sheep and corn'. Sheep thrive on the high open land in Aldsworth and their dung fertilises the poor soil, enabling adequate crops of grain to be grown. A 1939 survey of the county of Gloucester puts the land in Aldsworth in the category of 'downland' with thin light soil for which a four-crop rotation of barley–turnips–arable–sheep is suitable. Agriculture was most successful in the parish when it was possible for sheep farming and crop growing to be organised to complement each other. This happened in the

Middle Ages when wool was the most important product;
and again in the nineteenth century when live sheep for
export as breeding stock, and sheep for slaughter for meat, as
well as wool were sold. Disintegration of the market for wool
ended the first period of prosperity and a fall in the price of
grain the second.

From 1743 to 1845 there was a racecourse 1 mile from the
village on the downs at the south-east of the parish, which
until the late eighteenth century stretched all the way to
Burford. The race meetings were very fashionable and for
many years at the turn of the century were attended by the
Prince of Wales, later King George IV. A stabling business and
a racehorse training stable flourished during this time, as did
the village inn.

In the nineteenth century the population was twice as great
as it is today, partly because of the racecourse, but mainly
because farming was then very profitable and supported
many people. For most of the last 1,000 years, however, the
population has been much the same size as it is today.

For nearly all of the first 500 years of the millennium the
village was controlled by large religious institutions. Already
by 1086 St Peter's of Gloucester held the largest estate in
Aldsworth; and, centuries before, the church in Bibury had
been granted land in Aldsworth to support a chapel. From
1151 the three estates in the village were held by St Peter's
Abbey, Gloucester; Oseney Abbey, Oxford; and Cirencester
Abbey. Their efficient organisation of wool production,
preparation and packaging, and consistent quality control
must have contributed greatly to the willingness of foreign
merchants to pay high prices for Cotswold wool. The profits
of this trade went to pay for the beautiful churches built in
the area. Only a general history of these 500 years can be
given, as nothing is known of the people who actually lived
in the village then.

In the second half of the millennium, significant times in
the history of the village were: the dissolution of the
monasteries in 1539 when a new class of landowner was

created; the Civil War of 1641–45 when Aldsworth suffered from being on the main route between the Royalist headquarters in Oxford and the Parliamentarian stronghold of Cirencester, resulting in a fall in its population; the starting up of annual horseracing on the downs stretching from Aldsworth to Burford in 1743; the enclosure of the land in 1793; the end of horseracing and the increased influence of the Church at the beginning of the Victorian era; the profitability of farming in the mid-nineteenth century, which led to increased prosperity all round and a rise in population; the long agricultural depression that followed, which, except for the time of the Great War 1914–18, lasted for sixty years; the Second World War 1939–45 when what the village had to offer – production of food, and open spaces for airfields where pilots could be trained to fly and fight – was valued again, and when the stimulus of new society in the form of soldiers, airmen and evacuees made this for many the happiest time of their lives in spite of the hardships; the mechanisation of farming in the 1940s and 1950s with the consequent disappearance of jobs, shops, services, school and people, leading on the one hand to a general sense of loss for many, but on the other hand to prosperity for those still occupied in farming, and opportunities for newcomers to enjoy life in a country village. In the last twenty years there has been a greater turnover of population than ever before as houses have been bought and sold. At the end of the millennium the long-awaited village hall was built.

Several families have had a great influence on the village in the last 500 years. The Duttons of Sherborne acquired the main estate in the village after the dissolution of the monasteries. The head of that family became a baronet in 1678 and a baron in 1784. From the 1790s Lord Sherborne controlled all of Aldsworth except for about 200 acres, and his grip on the parish was strengthened by the Enclosure Act of 1793. His successor still owned a significant part of Aldsworth in 1982 when the estate was left to the National Trust. Most of the property in Aldsworth was then sold.

Members of the Waine family came to Aldsworth, from nearby, in about 1700 when the population was small, and they played a prominent role in the following 200 years. They were maltsters, bakers, brewers and stable keepers as well as farmers.

The Garne family came to Aldsworth in 1800 as tenant farmers of the large newly enclosed farms. They became renowned for breeding sheep and cattle. Their success in the prosperous mid-nineteenth-century years carried them through the difficult times for farming which followed.

In the twentieth century the Phillips family had a great influence on the village. John Phillips came to the area as a child of 4 years old in 1891 when his family migrated from Cornwall to Gloucestershire. In the 1930s he took on many farms in and around Aldsworth and elsewhere in the county. His son Gregory lived and farmed in Aldsworth for more than 50 years from 1946.

PART I

Before 1000

BRITAIN has been inhabited since the last ice age. The burial mounds known as barrows dating from 3000 to 2000 BC provide the earliest evidence of human habitation in Aldsworth. A map of 1777 shows that there were once seven barrows in the south-east of the parish. One, Ladbarrow, is still marked on maps, though there is nothing to see there today. There must also have been one of these mounds at Cocklebarrow, but no trace remains. Near Ladbarrow Farm is the site of an iron-age fort dating from about 800 BC and evidence of Celtic fields from the same era.

The area was well populated in Roman times. Aldsworth is 10 miles from Cirencester, which was the second largest city of Roman Britain. Roman roof tiles and fragments of pottery and building materials have been found in the parish near Cocklebarrow Farm, near Wall Farm and near Larket Hill.

After the Roman legions left Britain in AD 410 the population of Britain fell. Cities were gradually deserted and people returned to live on sites on high ground where they could defend themselves and their property. It is possible that Wall Farm was such a settlement, and it may have had a wall round it, which would account for its unusual name. It would account too for the name of the village. 'Aldsworth' is usually interpreted as coming from the Anglo-Saxon words *Eald* meaning 'old', and *worth* meaning 'enclosure', indicating that when the Anglo-Saxons arrived they found there was already a settlement. Recently it has been suggested that the name could mean the enclosure of someone called 'Eald' – but there is no record of anyone ever being called by that name.

The part of England containing Aldsworth was settled in about AD 600 by a tribe called the Hwicce of mixed Anglian and Saxon descent who gave their name to the forest of Wychwood, remnants of which remain to the east of the parish. The territory of the Hwicce, which covered the area of

Gloucestershire, Worcestershire and part of Warwickshire, became an under-kingdom of the Anglo-Saxon kingdom of Mercia. The earliest record of the name 'Ealdeswyrth' is in 1004, when land in Aldsworth was granted to Burton Abbey, Staffordshire, which in 1008 exchanged it for land nearer the abbey.

Anglo-Saxon England was converted to Christianity in the seventh century, and by 680 the bishopric of Worcester had been created for the Hwicce by Archbishop Theodore. An important Minster church was established at Bibury in the next century, and this acted as a mission station converting the area around it. Three dependant chapels were set up, one of which was in Aldsworth. The Christian Church brought reading and writing to the illiterate Anglo-Saxons, and links with the wider world. By the year 1000 England was a well-ordered and prosperous country united under one king.

Domesday

IN 1000 England was again under threat from the Danes, as it had been in the time of King Alfred 125 years before, and from 1018 to 1035 it had a Danish king, Canute. The kingdom then went back to the descendants of the Anglo-Saxon kings, but after the death of Edward the Confessor in 1066, the succession was disputed. William of Normandy claimed the throne, and conquered England after defeating King Harold at Hastings in that year.

Twenty years later, in Gloucester in 1085, King William told his counsellors of his plan to make a survey of the whole of England. This was completed within a year and all the information fair copied into the *Domesday Book*, a single book of two volumes that still exists. It records the size of each estate in the kingdom and what it was worth in taxes; the number of ploughs; and the number of villagers, smallholders and slaves. It also recorded who held each estate in 1086 and who had held it before the Conquest, so that any disputes could be settled. The investigation was carried out very thoroughly, so we know the information is correct. Almost all of England was included. In the area around Aldsworth all the present-day villages are included in *Domesday Book* and there are no villages in it which have disappeared, so the pattern of settlement was very similar to what it is today.

There were three estates or 'manors' in Aldsworth at the time the *Domesday Book* was compiled in 1086.

One estate of 2 hides was held by one of the King's thanes, Alfward son of Reinbald. This estate was 'at Wall', in other words at Wall Farm. (One hide was about 120 acres.)

A second estate, of 11 hides, was held by St Peter's of Gloucester.

A third estate, of 3 hides, was held by a priest in Bibury, and has been identified fairly recently as 'the rectory manor of Bibury and Aldsworth'. This was land in Aldsworth belonging to the church in Bibury, given to it to support its chapel in Aldsworth.

These three estates, Wall Farm, Aldsworth Manor and the Rectory Manor, kept their separate identities until the mid-twentieth century.

The population in 1086 was probably larger than it is today.

Local government and land

THE Normans took over from the Anglo-Saxons a well-organised country with an efficient system of law and local government.

The country was divided into the shires or counties we know today. Each shire was divided into hundreds. Representatives from 100 hides of land would assemble at a known meeting place in the open air every four weeks to

settle disputes and make decisions. Bibury was so important
at this time that it had its own hundred, and in 1086
Aldsworth was part of this. The meeting place was at Bibury
Elms. Later Aldsworth became part of Brightwells Barrow
Hundred, the meeting place for which was Barrow Elm near
Hatherop. It is interesting that these sites, where there have
never been any buildings or permanent landmarks, were so
important that they are still marked on Ordnance Survey
maps today.

All land in England belonged to the king. Each estate was
held by a thane or lord in return for duties or payments.
Originally the thane supplied the king and his court with
goods and produce, and supplied armed men in time of
trouble. He also had to maintain bridges and highways. Later
tax was paid instead, but the *Domesday Book* records that
payments in kind were still due in parts of Gloucestershire –
honey, salt, malt, cows, pigs and 'loaves for dogs' among
other things.

The villagers held land from their lord in return for labour
services such as ploughing, haymaking, sheep shearing,
harvesting and carting, and were not allowed to leave their
lord's estates. There were smallholders too, owing dues and
services. The Anglo-Saxons used ploughs drawn by a team of
eight oxen. If one family kept each pair of oxen, four families
had to co-operate to plough. Because turning the plough
round was difficult, fields were large and unfenced, and
decisions about their cultivation were made in common. A
hide was reckoned to be the amount of land that could be
cultivated by a plough-team over a year, and a quarter of this,
called a yard-land, was the share of each household. In this
area a hide was about 120 acres. From this basis medieval
farming and local government evolved. As time went on,
many of the customary dues and services were changed to
rent or taxes. Many different types of tenancy evolved.
Tenants had rights as well as duties. Much of the land was
uncultivated common land over which various people had
various rights – the right to graze animals, to collect furze for

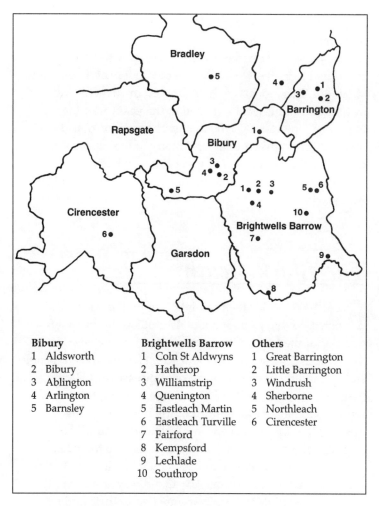

Bibury	Brightwells Barrow	Others
1 Aldsworth	1 Coln St Aldwyns	1 Great Barrington
2 Bibury	2 Hatherop	2 Little Barrington
3 Ablington	3 Williamstrip	3 Windrush
4 Arlington	4 Quenington	4 Sherborne
5 Barnsley	5 Eastleach Martin	5 Northleach
	6 Eastleach Turville	6 Cirencester
	7 Fairford	
	8 Kempsford	
	9 Lechlade	
	10 Southrop	

Map showing the hundreds in south-east Gloucestershire in 1086

fire wood or to hunt game, for example. The whole system was very complicated.

In 1133 Henry I granted Wall Farm to the Augustinian Abbey of St Mary in Cirencester, which he had recently founded.

In 1151 the Augustinian Abbey at Oseney, Oxford, took over Bibury Church and its properties. It seems that the early religious foundations called Minsters, such as that at Bibury, had undergone a decline.

The largest estate in the village, 'Aldsworth Manor', continued to be held by St Peter's of Gloucester. Founded in about 681, this monastery had adopted the Benedictine rule in 1022 and underwent a revival in the years after the Norman Conquest. By 1100 the number of monks had increased from two to sixty and many of the estates it had lost in the late Saxon period had been won back.

For nearly 400 years these three monasteries controlled Aldsworth.

The Black Death

FROM 1066 to 1300 the population of England steadily increased to a peak of about 4¼ million. In the first few decades of the fourteenth century, the climate changed dramatically, becoming cold and wet. Harvests failed, people starved and there were outbreaks of disease. In 1348 the plague known as the Black Death swept through Europe, rapidly killing about one-third of the population. It is possible that in the area around Aldsworth half of the population died. Further outbreaks of disease followed.

The dramatic decrease in population had an effect on the social order. Labour became scarce and wages shot up. It became impossible to keep peasants tied to their lord's estates. There is an example of this in Aldsworth in 1412 when eight unfree tenants were said to have fled and the abbey to have seized all of its bondsmen's goods and chattels. The lords themselves broke the law by employing peasants from other estates. It became impossible to enforce labour services and customary dues and over time they were replaced by cash rents. In the fields, survivors annexed vacant plots and farmed them with their own. They were able to acquire more security of tenure. Many more tenants held land by copy-hold – that is, for a term of three lives – which meant they could pass their holdings on to their sons. A few former tenants came to hold their property freehold.

By the early sixteenth century the abbeys let their estates instead of farming them themselves. Gloucester Abbey let its arable land in Aldsworth in 1514 and its flocks of sheep totalling 600 in 1532. All three estates in Aldsworth were let by 1536.

The wool trade

WOOLLEN rugs and cloaks were among the most prized exports from Britain in Roman times. The damp and moderate British climate provides grazing all the year round. The gentle hills of the Cotswolds are particularly suited to sheep rearing. At some stage the distinctive long-fleeced Cotswold breed with its shaggy forelock evolved.

In the Middle Ages the great abbeys dominated the wool trade in the Cotswolds. In 1306 the Abbey of St Peter in Gloucester had 10,000 sheep. The wool produced was mostly exported, mainly to Flanders but also to Italy. It went by packhorse through the staple at Calais; or, in the case of wool for Italy, to London for a mainly overland journey, or to Southampton for a voyage all the way by sea. The wool trade reached a peak around 1300 when wool exports (1304–11) from England averaged 39,000 sacks a year, each sack containing at least 250 fleeces. In 1350–60 an average of 32,000 sacks a year were exported; but in 1390–99 an average of only 19,000. However, during that half-century exports of woollen cloth from England increased from 5,000 to 35,000 cloths a year (cloths made in Italy at that time were about 26 yards long).

The correspondence of Francesco di Marco Datini, a merchant of Prato, near Florence, between 1382 and 1410 makes clear that the finest and most expensive wool at that time was from England. It cost at least twice as much as wool from all other countries (except wool from Minorca, which was four-fifths of the price of the English). This wool went to make the finest cloth, dyed gorgeous colours with products imported to Italy from far-flung lands. The wool from the 'Chondisgualdo' (Cotswolds) was especially prized, particularly that from 'Norleccio' (Northleach), 'Boriforte' (Burford) and 'Siricestri' (Cirencester), although 'Guincestri' (Winchester) is also mentioned.

Aldsworth was at the epicentre of this Cotswolds wool-producing area. Sheep from the main estate at Aldsworth were probably driven to Northleach to be washed and sheared together with the flocks from Gloucester Abbey's estates around that town, and the wool sold in its huge open market. The wool from the Cirencester Abbey estate of Wall Farm probably went to Cirencester. Wool from Oseney Abbey's estate at the Manor could have gone to Burford. Demand was such that purchasers sometimes bought the wool in advance, sight unseen, from the great abbeys; but, according to a letter to the merchant in Italy from a wool-buying firm, the very best time to buy wool was around the feast of St John, on 24 June, when the big Cotswold Fairs were held – appropriately, for one of the symbols of St John the Baptist is a lamb.

The great abbeys grew rich from the wool trade, not only from the profits from their own flocks but also from tithes payable on wool produced by others. The wool merchants in the towns also grew rich. The wealth went to pay for the magnificent churches built in the Cotswolds at that time.

Aldsworth Church in the Middle Ages

IT is not known who built, or rather rebuilt, Aldsworth Church between 1350 and 1500 – probably all three abbeys of Oseney, Gloucester and Cirencester contributed. The result can be seen today, as far as the exterior of the church is

concerned. However, the interior would then have looked
quite different. There would have been statues, shrines,
candles, paintings, stained glass and a rood screen: that is, a
large screen between the nave and the chancel surmounted
by a crucifix or calvary. There would probably also have been

Aldsworth Church

music, since Oseney Abbey was bound by its rule to choral celebration of divine office. The church played a dominant role in the life of the people in the Middle Ages. In an age before printed calendars and diaries, let alone radio, television or daily newspapers, people relied on church services to keep track of the seasons of the year, the days of the week, even the time of day. Important dates when payments were made, meetings held or ploughing, sowing or harvesting due, were marked by feasts of the church, such as Lady's Day, Lammastide, Michaelmas, All Hallows and Christmas. Letters were often dated by a saint's day or other day in the church calendar rather than by the day of the month. Church courts had jurisdiction over wills, payment of debts and tithes, as well as moral transgressions. The church provided education and welfare for the poor.

The monasteries

FROM 1151 when Bibury Church and its properties were taken over by Oseney Abbey in Oxford, until 1539, a period of nearly 400 years, the three abbeys of St Peter in Gloucester, St Mary in Cirencester and Oseney Abbey in Oxford held all of Aldsworth.

The great abbeys of England held much of the land, including one-third of Gloucestershire. By the 1530s it was widely felt that they had outlived their usefulness. The invention of printing meant that books could be made available to all, doing away with the need for monks in scriptoria copying out religious texts by hand. The charitable work that the monasteries undoubtedly did was deemed insufficient to justify their enormous wealth. Since the time of Wyclif and the Lollards in the fourteenth century, the clergy in general and monks in particular had been resented and criticised for their greed. They were regarded as venal for preying on the gullible by charging large sums of money for supposed relics of saints, for signed pieces of paper called indulgences, and for masses for the dead, all of which, it was claimed, could shorten the aeons of suffering in purgatory to be endured by the purchaser or his departed loved ones. The reformers, now able to read the Bible for themselves, questioned the existence of purgatory.

In addition the Pope in Rome was claiming too much power, not only over religious institutions but also over the political affairs of other rulers. So there were many reasons for the monasteries to be abolished besides Henry VIII's desire to divorce his queen, and his need to increase his royal revenues.

The wealthiest abbey in England was Westminster with an annual income of £3,471 0s 2¼d, but the abbeys of Gloucestershire were also wealthy. Gloucester Abbey's annual income was £1,946 5s 9d, that of Cirencester Abbey £1,156 9s 9¼d.

The dissolution of the monasteries

THE smaller monasteries were dissolved in 1536, the larger in 1539, and their wealth was surrendered to the King. Gold and silver ornaments were melted down and other valuables sold. Books and records were destroyed. In most cases the monastic buildings were demolished or damaged beyond repair. Nothing remains of Cirencester Abbey's buildings; Oseney Abbey has also disappeared. However, the magnificent abbey church of St Peter in Gloucester, built for the Benedictine monks between 1072 and 1499, survived. It became Gloucester Cathedral, the seat of the new diocese of Gloucester.

Most of the monasteries' great estates, which often spread over many counties, and which had supplied most of their income, now belonged to the crown. However, over the next century most of this land was sold and thus a whole new class of landowner was created.

In Gloucestershire the crown granted a lease of Aldsworth Manor, formerly held by Gloucester Abbey, to Thomas Dutton of Sherborne in 1577. In 1611 his son William bought the freehold.

The Cirencester Abbey estate of Wall Farm was granted in 1543 to Richard Andrews and Nicholas Temple. In 1547 it was sold by Richard to William Blomer of Cowley.

Oseney Abbey's estate in Aldsworth was granted in 1546 to Christ Church, Oxford. It was leased to John Blomer of Heythrop. Later a lease was granted in 1560 to Edward Barnard, gentleman of London.

The age of Queen Elizabeth I

THOMAS Dutton (1507–81) of Westwell had bought Sherborne Manor in 1551 from Sir John Allen, Lord Mayor of London. It had formerly belonged to Winchcombe Abbey. The abbot himself used to stay in Sherborne every year to supervise the shearing of the abbey's flocks of sheep, totalling nearly 3,000, and there was already an important house there called The Grange.

Thomas also acquired land in Windrush, Northleach, Bourton-on-the-Water, Wick Rissington, Brockhampton, Sevenhampton and Clapton. The fact that he had been created Surveyor of Crown Lands in Gloucestershire must have helped. His only son William (1561–1618) added Aldsworth Manor and Northleach Manor, and so much other property that he could boast of being able to ride from Sherborne to Cheltenham without leaving his own land. He also acquired Standish, a large and important manor near Gloucester.

In 1575 Queen Elizabeth I came to stay with Thomas Dutton at Sherborne Grange. Again in 1592, during her second progress through Gloucestershire, the Queen came to stay for six days with William Dutton.

Queen Elizabeth was an expert horsewoman, fond of hunting, hawking and coursing of deer with greyhounds. It is said that in her seventieth year she rode 10 miles to a hunt. It is likely that during her visits to Sherborne she would have ridden with her hosts through Aldsworth to the Seven Downs, ideal for hunting, hawking and horseracing. The second visit was four years after the glorious defeat of the Spanish Armada. No doubt the matter was discussed at the dinner table.

The early seventeenth century

WHEN William Dutton died in 1618 he left Standish Manor to his youngest son Ralph and the Sherborne Estate to his son John (1594–1656).

John Dutton, known as Crump because he was a hunchback, thus became one of the largest landowners and the wealthiest commoner in Gloucestershire. Indeed he was one of the richest men in England. In his youth he studied law and inclined to Puritanism. He represented Gloucestershire in Parliament as knight of the shire, and was to be seen at court, where his brother Ralph was a gentleman of the Privy Chamber. In the 1620s he supported Parliament in their disagreements with the King. He refused to pay the forced loan demanded by the King in 1626 or, as a JP, to collect it from others, and for this he was imprisoned.

From 1629 for ten years, King Charles I ruled without Parliament, but in 1640 another parliament was called. John Dutton was at first counted as a parliamentary supporter, but as matters grew more serious he absented himself from many important debates.

In early 1642, after his failed attempt to arrest five members of the House of Commons, Charles left London for the north and made his headquarters at York. The moment of decision had come.

The English Civil War

O N 22 August 1642 the Royal Standard was raised at
Nottingham, signalling the start of the Civil War.

Sir Ralph Dutton 'beat upon a drum' in Gloucestershire
and raised a regiment of 800 Royalist soldiers: he was
arrested by the Parliamentarians but escaped by plunging
into the Severn and swimming to the other side to join his
regiment, which was one of the first to join the King at
Nottingham. Later he died while trying to escape from
Scotland to France in 1646.

His brother John Dutton was more cautious. He offered
the King £50,000 at the outbreak of war. He joined the King
for a while in Oxford, which was made the Royalist
headquarters on 29 October 1642. He contributed '30 steel
back and breast plates with helmets, and two men and
horses completely armed' in early 1643 when a Royalist
regiment was being raised. After the first battle of the war
at Edgehill on 23 October 1642, which was inconclusive,
some Royalist troops are said to have come to Sherborne
House, ransacked it and burnt it down. This would have
made John Dutton's support for the Royalists somewhat
lukewarm. However, during 1643 it proved impossible for
him to refuse to pay large sums to establish and support the
Royalist garrisons at Cirencester, Sudeley and Tewkesbury,
and he even became one of the Royalist commissioners in
charge of this.

When two months after the start of the war King Charles I
had moved his headquarters to Oxford, one of his main aims
was to capture the Parliamentarian strongholds of Bristol,
Cirencester and Gloucester in order to open his lines of
communication with the Royalist west and with Wales.

Aldsworth, being right on the road between Oxford and
Cirencester, could not help but be affected by the campaigns
of 1643. Those in the village with family or business
connections in Cirencester may have volunteered to help in

its defence, or been coerced into doing so. Most of the inhabitants of the village would necessarily have taken the same stance as their landlord.

In January 1643 some of the Parliamentarian forces in Cirencester successfully raided Royalist troops at Burford. Prince Rupert retaliated. He failed to capture Cirencester, but at a second attempt on 2 February, Cirencester was taken by storm. A thousand prisoners were taken and imprisoned overnight in the church. The next day, the people of Aldsworth could have seen the survivors being marched along the road to prison in Oxford with no shoes or stockings, and many with no outer clothing to protect them from the wintry weather.

During the campaign to capture Cirencester, Royalist troops plundered the villages round the town, ate up all the provisions, spoiled corn and hay, took all the horses, sheep, oxen and other cattle, and sent 200 cartloads of plunder to Oxford. The Royalist commissioners wrote to the King in March to say that it was difficult to collect taxes in the hundreds around Cirencester because 200–300 horses had been taken from local villages, so that they could not sow their fields, which left the land lying waste. 'Dearth' and a shortfall of taxes in the future were predicted.

In April, Cirencester was abandoned by the Royalists because of the cost of maintaining the garrison, and re-occupied by the Parliamentarians; in September, it was captured again by the Royalists. There must have been constant activity along the road past Aldsworth. No doubt soldiers came into the village, requisitioned supplies and billeted themselves in the houses. Payment was supposed to be made for this, but was not always forthcoming immediately, if at all. Troops marching to and fro would have recruited men for soldiers along the way. In addition, the Royalists introduced impressment in Gloucestershire in 1644. Perhaps men from Aldsworth went willingly: there cannot have been much left at home to stay for. Some may have been killed or wounded.

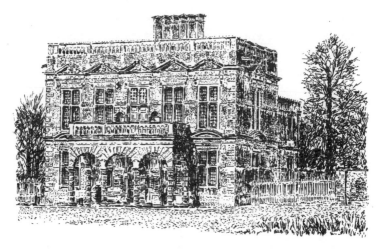

Lodge Park

In January 1645 a further force of 1,500 Royalist infantry arrived in Cirencester. In May the King left Oxford for Chester. On 11 June the Royalists were defeated at the battle of Naseby. Now it was the turn of the New Model Army to be seen in the Cotswolds. They camped at Chipping Camden, Northleach and Lechlade on their way west to Bath and Bristol. It was probably at this time that Parliamentarian soldiers ransacked the church in Aldsworth and destroyed the statues, paintings and ornaments. Someone must have preserved some of the fifteenth-century stained glass: fragments of it were later made into a window in the south porch.

In March 1646 the Royalist forces at Cirencester left to join up with those coming from Wales, but these forces were routed at Stow-on-the-Wold. The New Model Army marched on Oxford. The first Civil War was over.

John Dutton was a commissioner of the Treaty of Oxford in 1646. He pleaded that he had been coerced into supporting the Royalist cause. He managed to keep his estates on payment of a large fine – and some extra for attempting to conceal the extent of his wealth. He then became a great friend of Oliver Cromwell, with whom he shared a love of hunting. When John Dutton died in 1566 he appointed Oliver Cromwell guardian of his heir, his nephew William, son of Sir Ralph Dutton of Standish.

The new government introduced reforms to the Church. The Sabbath was to be strictly observed. The Church of England prayer book was banned. Celebration of Christmas, Easter, Whitsun and other feasts of the Church was forbidden. All this as well as the desecration of their church must have been very upsetting for many people in Aldsworth. No doubt, like most of the rest of the nation, they were heartily glad to have the monarchy restored and the prayer book reinstated in 1660.

It is possible that Aldsworth took several generations to recover from the Civil War. The population in 1712 was said to be about 120. This is the figure given by Robert Atkyns, Kt, a Gloucestershire man, in his book *The Ancient and Present State of Gloucestershire*. Bad harvests, plague and other epidemics may have helped to keep the population low.

The house now called Aldsworth Manor was built in the mid-seventeenth century, the old house being described as 'quite ruinated and not habitable'. Green Farm House is said to have been built in 1700, though there must have been a house there before. Maybe it was derelict. Other buildings may also have been damaged or destroyed during the Civil War.

The Waine family

THE first person of the name Waine recorded in Aldsworth is John Waine (1664–1730), who was 'yeoman builder of Green Farm Estate Manor House circa 1700', according to Waine family records, though obviously there was a house there originally. His ancestors can be traced back in direct line to William Waine (1530–83), who lived in Great Barrington.

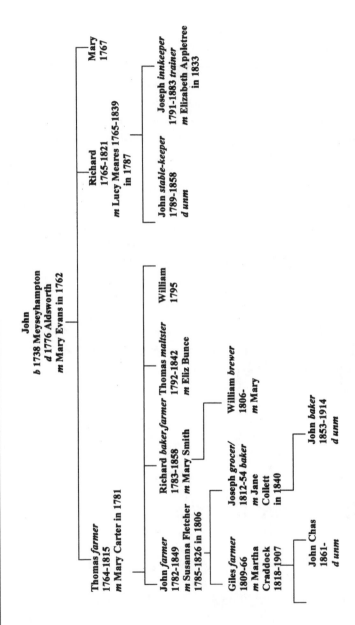

Family tree of the Waine family in Aldsworth (omitting details of daughters, sons who left the village and sons who died young)

This first John was born in Fairford but died in Aldsworth. He was married to Mary Evans. According to parish records their four children, Ann, John, Thomas and Giles, were born in Hatherop between 1690 and 1700, but the three sons were buried in Aldsworth. The eldest son John, born in 1691, died in 1731 just one year after his father, leaving one daughter and no son. The second son Thomas, born in 1693, may then have taken over Green Farm, of which the family were tenants. In 1766, three years after Thomas died, his son John (1738–76) bought Green Farm, which was a freehold property of about 200 acres.

John's uncle Giles, born in 1700, may have lived as sub-tenant at the Rectory Manor Farm where a John Waine had been recorded in 1712. Giles died in 1771, leaving two daughters but having outlived his two sons. A year later in 1772 John acquired a lease of the Rectory Manor direct from Christ Church.

All the Waines who subsequently lived in Aldsworth – and there were many – were descended from this John Waine, who was born in Meyseyhampton in 1738 and died and was buried in Aldsworth in 1776.

At the time the Waines came to Aldsworth the population was small – about 120 – but it increased greatly during the eighteenth century. By 1801 it was 280. The Waines themselves multiplied. John (1738–76) had two sons and a daughter. In the next generation, thirteen with the surname Waine were born in Aldsworth; in the following generation thirty-six – most of them in Aldsworth.

The family played a dominant role in the village in the eighteenth and early nineteenth centuries. In the eighteenth century the Waine family had a malthouse where barley was spread out to sprout and then dried to make malt. In those days many householders would buy malt to brew beer at home. Malt was also widely used as a sweetener – for baking, with cereals, and for milk drinks. The Waine family also had a bakehouse, on a different site from Green Farm. Here bread would have been baked and also, perhaps, Sunday dinners cooked for those who did not have an oven of their own at home. It seems that the Waines also had a profitable stabling business.

In the following century one member of the family was a tenant farmer, farming 400 acres of the Rectory Manor Estate belonging to Christ Church. Another set up a grocer's shop, which by 1851 had become the village bakery. Meanwhile the family bakehouse had, by 1841, been turned into a brewery, run by members of the Waine family. Finally one member of the family was a racehorse trainer, and later an innkeeper. Thus the Waines were, variously, farmers, maltsters, bakers, brewers, stable keepers and racehorse trainers, innkeepers and grocers. That they were prosperous as well as resourceful is shown by the thirty-two fine inscribed gravestones that they left in the churchyard. The earliest with a legible inscription ('Ann Waine 1743') is a fine tabletop monument, probably a family tomb.

John died aged only 37 in 1776 when his children were aged 13, 11 and 9. He left Green Farm to his son Thomas (1764–1815), and some other property not identifiable to his younger son (1765–1821). His wife Mary Evans took over the lease of the Rectory Manor Farm, which she held until 1791.

The early eighteenth century

A T the beginning of the eighteenth century, the tenants of the Rectory Manor Farm belonging to Christ Church were the Powle family of Williamstrip Manor near Coln St Aldwyns, who had held a lease of it since 1612. Probably it was sub-let and none of them actually lived in Aldsworth.

Wall Farm had belonged since 1686 to the Webb family of Hatherop Manor.

The lord of the main manor in Aldsworth was Sir Ralph Dutton of Sherborne, who had succeeded his brother William, ward of Oliver Cromwell, in 1675. He had been made a baronet in 1678 by Charles II in tribute to his father's support of the Royalist cause. Sir Ralph was apparently a gambler with no aptitude for business affairs and already by 1709, before his death, his son John, born in 1682, a staunch Hanoverian, had taken on the running of the estate, which prospered during his time.

This was the age of enlightenment when the new ideas of science were being applied to agriculture as well as industry. Already in the 1660s the Royal Society had formed a committee for agriculture. Owners of large estates had started experimenting with new breeds of animals, new methods of cultivation and new crops such as turnips for winter fodder and nitrogenous crops such as clover to improve the soil; and had begun comparing results with their neighbours.

The early eighteenth century was a time of peace and prosperity at home. The 1680s had been uneasy years dominated by fears of a Catholic succession to the throne and by Monmouth's rebellion, and after James II's succession to the throne by further rebellion and war until he was replaced as monarch by William and Mary in the 'Glorious Revolution' of 1689. The 1690s had seen bad harvests and famine. But by 1730 the population of England was growing again. In Aldsworth the population rose from 120 in 1712 to 288 at the end of the century.

However, it was not only peace at home and the efficient running of the farms that caused the population of Aldsworth to grow. There was also the racecourse.

The racecourse

FOR eighty-three years from 1743 to 1825 race meetings were held every year on the Seven Downs near Ladbarrow, on the boundaries of the three parishes of Aldsworth, Eastleach and Little Barrington. The ground there is particularly suited to horseracing. The area must have been one of special significance in prehistoric times as there were seven barrows there. It was the Burford races that were held at the racecourse from 1743 to 1802, but the course was 4 or 5 miles from the town of Burford, whereas it was only 1 mile from the village of Aldsworth.

Burford races were recorded intermittently in the early seventeenth century. In 1681 a grand and fashionable race meeting was held while Parliament was sitting in Oxford. The memory of this glorious occasion, when King Charles II and his courtiers had come to Burford and attended the races 'on the long plain adjoining', lingered long in the minds of many in the town who hoped that such an event would be repeated. The troubled political situation made this impossible and Charles II died in 1685.

There followed an interval of sixty years with no racing. In 1743 the time was right. To get racing started up again it would have been necessary to have the support of the major landowners in the area. Sir John Dutton had died in 1742 and his heir, a nephew from Ireland, James Lenox Naper, who had agreed to take the name of Dutton on succeeding to the Sherborne Estate, was obviously a racing enthusiast. The race meetings, which were held once or twice a year and were up to six days long, were important ones in the racing calendar, and were attended by royalty, the nobility and all the important people in the racing world. They were also important social occasions for people living in the area.

Enclosure

THE new ideas for farming could not be easily put into practice where, as in Aldsworth, most of the land was held in common in open fields and unfenced downs. To change this an Act of Parliament was necessary, since the rights of many people were involved. Much of the midlands of England was enclosed in this way in the eighteenth century. The 'Inclosure'

Act for Aldsworth was passed in 1793. It was required by law
that a map showing the changes made should be drawn and
kept in a safe place. It is fortunate that the Aldsworth Estate
Map, dated 1799, has survived, as many have not. It shows the
result of the enclosure in great detail, though it is difficult to get
from it a mental picture of what the land looked like before.

Before enclosure no one had absolute rights over any piece
of land: even lords of the manor held strips of land in open
fields, decisions about which were made communally. Over
almost any piece of land held by one person others had
rights: the right to graze sheep on the stubble, the right to
catch rabbits, the right to collect firewood.

A further problem was that individuals held plots of land
that were widely separated from one another. For instance, in
Aldsworth Thomas Waine held 17 acres at the extreme north-
east of the parish by the road to Sherborne, a mile or two
from Green Farm. He also had a 2³/₄-acre site, a quarry, by the
side of the road near Larket Hill. William Peacey, who lived
in the village, had a 15-acre plot and an 11-acre plot between
Conygree and Larket Hill.

Once absolute right or freehold had been allotted to all the
land, it was possible for the owners to buy, sell or swap it free
of restrictions. Thus Lord Sherborne was able to exchange
Thomas Waines' 17 acres for land near Green Farm, to buy
William Peacey's 15 acres and to swap William Peacey's
11-acre site for 'Vineyard Close', presumably a site in the
village.

Of the 3,158 acres in Aldsworth affected by the enclosure,
Lord Sherborne was awarded 2,228 acres for his open field
land, tithes and common rights, and shared some land. The
Dean and Chapter of Christ Church were awarded 590 acres
for their glebe and tithes, the curate 26 acres for his tithes and
Thomas Waine 204 acres. By 1799 Lord Sherborne owned
2,417 acres and also held a lease of the Rectory Manor Estate.

Some areas of downland remained unenclosed. The east
downs at Ladbarrow, the site of the racecourse, had been
bought by Lord Sherborne by 1825. Blackpits Downs to the

north-west, and Allens Downs north of Wall Farm had been enclosed by 1839.

One benefit of enclosure in Aldsworth was that tithes were abolished. Originally payments made voluntarily, as described in the Bible, for charitable works, they were made compulsory by the early Anglo-Saxon kings and assigned to the newly established Christian Church. They soon became just another tax. After dissolution the new owners of the monastic lands, such as the Duttons, took over the valuable tithes together with the lands. (In Aldsworth just a part of the tithes was assigned to be paid as a pension to the Bishop of Gloucester). In many parts of England tithes, paid to a lay lord of the manor, survived well into the twentieth century.

It is impossible to say whether anyone in Aldsworth suffered hardship as a result of the enclosure. There may have been some who could no longer keep a cow or a few sheep, who felt that a cash payment did not compensate them for the loss of rights on the common land. But certainly the enclosure brought benefits. It provided employment, for there were many walls to build round the newly enclosed fields. The roads were also realigned and rebuilt. The land became much more productive after enclosure: 470 extra acres were cultivated, yields of wheat, barley, oats and peas increased and the number of sheep trebled.

Stables, jockeys, racehorse trainers and the village inn

THE racecourse must have brought increased demand for stabling, fodder, food, drink and accommodation in the village of Aldsworth.

It is possible that there were stables run by the Waine family on the side of the main Cirencester–Burford road around the site of the present-day pub, the Sherborne Arms.

The 1799 enclosure map of the village marks a freehold plot of about ¼ acre on this site, 'House, messuage, garden and outbuildings', and gives the name of the freeholder as Richard Waine. The surrounding land was part of Green Farm. Some curiously shaped pieces of land with no buildings on them are shown on the map – perhaps the stables were here? Richard Waine (1765–1821) must have lived here because his four children were born and baptised in Aldsworth between 1787 and 1794, and because the tenants of all the other houses in the village are named, so it is difficult to see where else he could have lived. Richard, who was the brother of Thomas Waine of Green Farm, had a son John (1789–1858) who was described in 1841 as a stable keeper. It is possible that Richard before him ran the business with the help of his brother and family at Green Farm.

The road past Aldsworth had been put in the charge of a turnpike trust in 1753 and improved. It was the main route from Cirencester to London before the coming of the railways in the 1840s. Fresh horses would have been needed for the coaches every 10 miles or so along the route. People in the village also would have needed to hire horses from time to time. The stable-keeping business was obviously a profitable

Taylers Farmhouse

one because John Waine (1789–1858), who apparently never married, became a rich man and in 1831 was able to build himself a fine three-storey house of cut ashlar stone with sash windows and slate roof in the shape of a pyramid, surrounded by a cornice and with a weathervane and his initials on top.

In 1851 this John Waine was described in the census of population as a landed proprietor with one servant-housekeeper and in *Kelly's Directory* of 1859 as a gentleman. The house he built replaced part of the former building on the site – the house and bakehouse belonging to Thomas Waine in 1799. It seems likely that John Waine bought the whole site from his cousins and invested in the brewery that replaced the bakery at about that time.

John's brother Joseph (1791–1883) had a long and varied career. In his youth he may have been a jockey. In the 1830s and 1840s he was a racehorse trainer, and at the end of his long life he was an innkeeper.

The 1799 enclosure map shows that the village inn, the Sherborne Arms, was then situated at the entrance to the village from the main Cirencester to Burford road: it was the first house on the left. The inn must have been very busy when the races were being held. An article in the *Oxford Journal* in 1797 announced that the forthcoming races would be held on 28 and 29 June and would include the race for the Burford Cup. It stated that all the runners would be shown at the Sherborne Arms in Aldsworth on the afternoon of the 27th. Nowadays racehorses are transported to the racecourse on the day of the race, sometimes by air from another country, but in the eighteenth century they would have had to be brought there the day before and stabled overnight. Presumably some were stabled in the 'Jockey stables' shown on the 1799 map next to the inn, but other stabling would probably have been needed. The piece of ground on the left of the road to Sherborne called 'Jockeys Hitching' would also have been used. All the lads who had walked the horses to Aldsworth would have needed accommodation, as would other visitors from afar. The inn must have been very crowded indeed before, during and after a race meeting. At other times it must have been busy too, accommodating travellers along the Cirencester to London road.

This inn was closed down in 1845. It is probable that it was completely demolished. The schoolteacher's house was built on the site in 1853.

Lord Sherborne and the Prince of Wales

SIR James Lenox Dutton had died in 1776 and been succeeded by his son James, who was made Baron Sherborne in 1784. By the time of the enclosure, Wall Farm had been acquired by Lord Sherborne. He also from 1793 held the lease of the Rectory Manor Estate, which he treated very much as his own. Thus except for the 204 acres owned by Thomas Waine and a few tiny plots, Lord Sherborne owned or controlled all of Aldsworth, and his successors continued to do so until the lease of the Rectory Manor Estate was given up in 1864 and Ladbarrow and Cocklebarrow Farms were sold in 1933 and 1949.

The First Lord Sherborne became a friend of the Prince of Wales, later George IV, and for many years, from 1792 to 1807, the Prince came every year to stay at Sherborne House and attend the Burford races. In fact because of his presence the Burford races became the Bibury Club races and only gentlemen were allowed to take part and ride the horses.

It seems that everyone got carried away by the presence of royalty. Throngs of fashionable people attended the races in those years. Lord Sherborne himself devised an ambitious plan to build a 'green' – that is, unpaved – carriageway direct from Sherborne House to the turnpike road. Provision for this was made in the 'Inclosure' Act; it was also to be a public bridlepath. The road was to go past Woeful Lake and Wall Farm Pool and emerge on the village green, and then to be driven straight through in front of the Rectory Manor House to the main road. The 1799 map shows the village before this road was completed and includes a number of cottages on the village green, which were in its path and had to be demolished. There was also a large pond to be drained.

It is unlikely that Lord Sherborne, having gone to all these lengths to build the carriage road, would have been content for it to end in a farmyard. It is more likely that he would have put into the Rectory Manor House, which he controlled, some of his own staff to greet him and his important guest when they arrived, and to serve them refreshments after their 3-mile drive; someone to wait with horses for them to mount to make their grand appearance on the racecourse on horseback; and someone, perhaps, in charge of their own racehorses – in other words, a racehorse trainer.

This trainer may have been one of the Sadler family. The Christ Church records show that a Thomas Sadler held 148 acres of the Rectory farmland in 1821. He may have been related to William Sadler, a successful racehorse trainer said to have lived in Aldsworth, who had at least a dozen horses in training in the years 1830–32, and who owned and trained Dangerous, the Derby winner of 1833. He is said to have left Aldsworth for Stockbridge in 1832.

After the Prince of Wales ceased to attend them, the Bibury Club races became somewhat less fashionable. The first Lord Sherborne died in 1820 and was succeeded by his son John. In 1826 the races were moved to Cheltenham, then to Stockbridge.

The years when the Prince of Wales came to Aldsworth were during the long war with France, which lasted on and off for twenty-five years from the French Revolution in 1789 to the defeat of Napoleon at Waterloo in 1815. There was widespread fear that revolution might spread to England, and that the country might be invaded. The militia were active in many parts of the land. The government asked for troops of volunteers to be raised in the shires. A troop of

'Yeomanry Cavalry' called 'Loyal Gloucester' was raised in 1796 in Northleach, which was part of Lord Sherborne's estate (see Appendix B). One can imagine that it might have been felt desirable for the 'Loyal Gloucester' to be on duty in the Aldsworth area at times when the Bibury Club race meetings were being held, in order to protect the heir to the throne. Perhaps the Prince and Lord Sherborne were accompanied on their carriage journey from Sherborne to Aldsworth by some of the troopers. If so, they must have looked fantastically smart in their uniforms, riding alongside the carriage. It is a shame no one was able to record the scene for us. The building on the lower green in Aldsworth known as 'The Barracks' may have been used as their headquarters.

Inflation and the disruption of trade caused by war, as well as bad harvests at the beginning of the century (particularly in the years 1799 and 1800, and 1808–12), drove up the price of corn, and therefore of bread, to record levels, the highest being in 1813 when corn was sold at £8.75 a quarter. The later war years and the first decades of the peace were a time of want and social unrest. Thirty-five Aldsworth people were receiving poor relief in 1803.

From 1736 the living of Aldsworth was held together with that of Turkdean, and there was generally no vicar resident in Aldsworth. It is said that during this time the sexton would keep a lookout in the belfry on Sunday mornings. Only when he saw the vicar coming along the road from Larket Hill did he ring the bells to summon the congregation to church. It is said that the bells were also rung when Dangerous won the Derby in 1833 at odds of 30/1.

The Garne family

THE first members of the Garne family to come to Aldsworth were William Garne (1743–1802), and his brother John (1753–1823), from Sherborne. In 1799 William took over Wall

Farm (280 acres) and John took over Ladbarrow Farm (600 acres). No doubt Lord Sherborne felt happy to have as tenants men he knew, and who had had experience of farming at Sherborne, where the land had been enclosed since 1777.

From 1799 until 1967 members of the Garne family farmed in Aldsworth. Twenty-four Garnes are buried in the churchyard. The full history of the Garne family has been ably told by Richard O. Garne in his admirable book *Cotswold Yeomen and Sheep*, a masterpiece of family and local history.

William Garne died in 1801. His widow and children continued to live in the farmhouse at Wall Farm and his eldest son William II (1781–1857), aged 19, took over the farming. Later he took over Blackpits (575 acres) and Conygree Farm (146 acres) – 1,054 acres in all. He was succeeded by his youngest son Robert, who farmed at Blackpits for forty-three years until his death in 1900. Robert, a bachelor, was succeeded by a nephew, W. T. Garne, who in turn was succeeded by his son Will in 1925.

At Ladbarrow John Garne was succeeded by his son Thomas, who farmed there until 1851 when he was succeeded by a nephew. But there were Garnes at Ladbarrow again from 1912 to 1934 when W. T. Garne's son Tom farmed there.

In addition, Arthur Garne, a distant cousin, came to Aldsworth in 1911 to help W. T. Garne. From 1918 to 1962 Arthur Garne held the tenancy of Cocklebarrow Farm.

The Garne family was blessed by fortune in being tenant farmers at a time of agricultural prosperity. This lasted until the 1880s, by which time they were wealthy and prosperous. Many had large families and many sons. The first William had nine children and so did the second. Three of William II's sons took on farms in Filkins, Kilkenny and Great Barrington. Other members of the family, such as William's brother Thomas and the latter's son George, became well-known and successful farmers.

These prosperous post-enclosure farmers concentrated on corn, sheep and cattle, leaving dairying, poultry and pig keeping to small holders in the villages. Many members of the Garne family became renowned nation-wide for breeding, showing, judging, selling and exporting Cotswold sheep. Others were renowned for their herds of shorthorn cattle, winning many prizes and awards. The last Garne to farm in Aldsworth, Will Garne (1880–1967), had the distinction of owning the very last flock of Cotswold sheep in England.

Two members of the family still live in Aldsworth and many others visit the village regularly.

Racing again

IN 1835 racing in Aldsworth started up again in the form of a spring meeting of the Bibury Club. This was a mistake on the part of Lord Sherborne. It was difficult to find enough prize money for racing at Ladbarrow while the club continued to have its main meeting at Stockbridge. Also it was no longer the noble, the rich, the famous and the fashionable who flocked to see the races, but people of quite a different order. In a report written in 1859, the full text of which is given in Appendix C, the vicar, the Revd John Bellingham, described the village at that time:

> 'Races were held in it, training stables supported which attracted a vast crowd of visitors of the lowest and most abandoned description. The public house was thronged on such occasions and pugilistic combats were encouraged and all kinds of games prevailed for the space of a whole week and caused considerable disorder and licentiousness among the parishioners.'

The shops were open on Sunday and there were 'Sunday games and sports and wrestling, boxing, cockfighting and cricketing … on the village green'.

The vicar was clearly appalled at the moral state of the parish he had taken on in 1839. A one-day meeting at the course at Aldsworth was recorded for the years 1835–45 and there was probably unofficial racing as well. Then in 1845 the vicar succeeded in 'abolishing the races, banishing the stable and suppressing the public house', and that was the end of racing at Ladbarrow.

The age of Queen Victoria

IN the 1830s and 1840s a profound change took place in the outlook and thinking of people in Britain. Attitudes, behaviour and pastimes that seemed quite normal in the Georgian and Regency ages became quite unacceptable. King William IV had been fairly respectable, but his brothers, particularly the Prince of Wales, who came to Aldsworth, became Regent in 1811 and reigned as King George IV from 1820 to 1830, had not. Even in his lifetime he had been criticised for keeping mistresses and being unkind to his wife, as well as for drinking, gambling and wild extravagance. Now there was a new young queen who, with her consort, had the highest standard of behaviour.

The beginning of change in Aldsworth can be dated to 1837, the very year that Queen Victoria ascended to the throne. In that year it was decided that Aldsworth should have its own vicar. In 1839 the Revd John Bellingham, a young man of 31 or 32, born in Madras, educated at Cambridge and ordained in London, was appointed by Christ Church, Oxford.

The records are rather hard to follow but it seems that the vicar did not immediately move into the Rectory Manor House close to the church, but in 1840 was appointed a house in Farmington until a glebe house had been built. This seems odd, because the Rectory House, having been in a state of ruin in 1835, was recorded as being completely restored in 1837, and as being empty in 1839. There was another house for the use of the tenant farmer of the land and the same tenant was farming the land in 1841 as in 1851. It also seems

odd that the racing stables should have been particularly
mentioned by the vicar in his report. One would have
thought that it would have been enough to stop the racing
and close the pub. Could it be, as seems possible, that the
racing stables were actually on the Rectory Manor Estate – in
fact right next to the house itself, so that from its upper
windows could be seen not only the cricket matches on the
village green but also the racehorses which John Bellingham
associated with drunkenness and licentiousness? This could
well be the reason that he did not move into the house, or
indeed the village, until after the races were stopped.

John Bellingham was vicar of Aldsworth for twenty-five
years. In 1851 he is recorded as living in the village with his
wife and two servants, and he probably spent much of the
following fourteen years there, although he is known to have
appointed curates, and an officiating minister was resident in
1861. It is interesting that, although an innkeeper was
recorded in the census of 1841, there was no innkeeper in
Aldsworth in 1851 or in 1861. Not until 1871, a few years
after the Revd John Bellingham had given up the living of
Aldsworth in 1865, was an innkeeper again recorded.

Collective amnesia settled over the village. By the
beginning of the next century, although it was known that a
well-known racehorse trainer had lived in Aldsworth, no one
could say for certain where he had lived, or where any stables
had been. Although it was known that the schoolteacher's
house had once been a pub, no one could tell its name.

We must be grateful to John Bellingham for succumbing to
an urge to record for posterity the situation in Aldsworth in
1839 and what he had done about it. On a routine printed
circular about college livings issued by the senior common
room of Christ Church in 1859, in addition to the brief
answers required, under heading 8, 'population', he penned
his marginal note. It must have taken a great deal of prayer,
persuasion and persistence to change things. It was a heroic
effort; but he had the spirit of the age, and no doubt many of
the parishioners, behind him.

John Bellingham would have been influenced by the Oxford Movement, which was a call to Anglicans to take their faith, and in particular their Church, more seriously. The Movement was supported from the start by many prominent people, including the great Mr Gladstone. John Bellingham may even have heard the sermon preached by John Keble in Oxford in 1833, which is said to have started the Movement. He would have read Keble's books and poems, which went through many editions. After his brilliant academic career, John Keble went home to act as curate to his father, who was vicar of Coln St Aldwyns, and he also served at Southrop and Eastleach. Though he left the area in 1836 he and John Bellingham may have met.

Between 1842 and 1877 the church in Aldsworth was thoroughly restored and rebuilt like many others up and down the land. It was mainly the clergy who were behind the changes introduced at that time, such as a surplice instead of a plain frock coat for the clergyman, and an altar instead of the plain communion table specified in the Book of Common Prayer.

Church attendance probably increased. From the inscriptions on tombs in the graveyard in Aldsworth it seems clear that there was more Bible reading. Early gravestones have simple inscriptions, but poems then became fashionable. On gravestones dated from 1816 to 1850 there are a dozen examples, usually expressing a deep faith in an elegant eighteenth-century manner, such as

'The hour of my departure's come
I hear his voice that calls me home
Not in my innocence I trust
I bow before him in the dust
And through my Saviour's blood alone
I look for mercy at his throne.'
Ann Mares, 1834

'Blame not. This monumental stone we raise
Is to the Saviour not the sinner's praise
Sin was the whole that she could call her own
Her goodness was derived from Him alone
To sin her conflicts pains and grief she owes
Her conquering faith and patience He bestows
Reader may'st thou obtain like precious faith
To smile in anguish and rejoice in death.'
Lucy Waine, 1839

or this for a child:

'How frail is beauty's bloom!
The dimpled cheek, the sparkling eye
Scarce seen before their wonders fly
To decorate a tomb.'
Eliza Peacey, 1841

There are no Bible quotations on gravestones before 1850, but between then and 1900 there are twenty quotations from the Bible, hymns or the prayer book – and only one poem. Examples of quotations are

'I know that my Redeemer liveth'
William Garne, 1857

'O Lamb of God that takest away the sins of the world have mercy upon us'
Pearcy Smith, 1862

'Suffer little children to come unto me and forbid them not for of such is the Kingdom of God'
Frederick Garne, 1865; Frank Houlton, 1875

'Be ye also ready for at such an hour as ye think not, the son of man cometh'
George Waine, 1870

'Take ye heed watch and pray for ye know not when the time is'
Lucy Houlton, 1882

It is probable that from the mid-nineteenth century onwards people in Aldsworth stayed at home on Sundays after going to church, and thought about their sins, and their responsibilities to God, to their families and to their neighbours. It is certain that there was no more shopping on a Sunday; that no one mentioned, or even thought about, cockfighting, or boxing or wrestling; and that there was no more cricket – at least not until, at the end of the century, it became a gentlemanly game, free of any suspicion of gambling or match-fixing.

The Waine family in the nineteenth century

T HE member of the Waine family who was most involved in horseracing in Aldsworth in 1845, the year that racing ceased, was Joseph Waine (1791–1883). In the years 1835–45 he was described as a 'training groom' – in other words, he was a racehorse trainer. Understandably, he and his wife and six children left Aldsworth in 1845. They moved to Cirencester where Joseph was a 'victualler'. The family returned to Aldsworth, probably in 1858 when Joseph's wealthy bachelor brother John, the stable keeper, died and they almost certainly moved then into the former family home on the main road. By 1871 Joseph was an innkeeper. Thus it was he who was the first innkeeper of the present-day Sherborne Arms – the second inn of that name in Aldsworth (see Part II: The Sherborne Arms).

At Green Farm, Thomas Waine (1764–1815) and his wife Mary had had six children who survived infancy. One daughter, Mary Ann, married William Garne in 1809; a granddaughter, Susanna, married W. T. Garne in about 1880; another daughter married and left. One son, Thomas, a maltster, moved out of the village in about 1830 and settled in

Burford. Another son, William, also left. Two sons lived all their lives in the village.

The second son of the family, Richard, was at first a baker, and then in the 1840s and 1850s farmed the Rectory Manor Farm. One of his sons was described as a baker in the 1830s, but by 1841 he was running the brewery that had replaced the family bakehouse; another son moved to Great Barrington.

The eldest son, John (1782–1849), succeeded his father Thomas at Green Farm in 1815. He and his wife Susanna had eleven children who survived infancy. One, Joseph, set up a shop in Aldsworth, which by 1851 was the village bakery: another, Giles, inherited the farm. But of the eleven, four married and left the village and five died unmarried.

None of the nine children of Joseph the innkeeper remained in the village. Gradually the number of people in Aldsworth with the surname Waine declined as the century advanced.

In 1897 Green Farm was sold and John Charles, the last Waine to farm there, moved away, leaving only his aged mother Martha behind. Then the only other Waines in the village were the last of the family at the bakery, John, his sister Elizabeth and two nephews. John and Elizabeth both died in 1914 and the bakery was sold not long afterwards. Now there are no Waines in Aldsworth, though there are many elsewhere (see Part II: Green Farm, The Manor, Taylers Farmhouse, The Old Bakery).

Education

By 1833 there were three small schools in Aldsworth in which children were educated at their parents' expense. There was also a Sunday school in the 1820s and 1830s supported by Lady Sherborne, which was attended by between fifty and sixty children. In 1847 there were two day schools with a total of fifty children.

Aldsworth Church of England School was built in 1853 by Lord Sherborne, who also provided a house rent-free for the teacher. Thirty-eight girls and twenty-four boys attended on weekdays; twenty-four girls and thirty-four boys on Sundays. Parents made a contribution only if they could afford it and the school was supported by voluntary contributions. But education was not yet compulsory. In 1861 there were in Aldsworth ten ploughboys and four agricultural labourers of the ages 9, 10, 11 and 12.

The average attendance at Aldsworth School up to 1900 was between fifty and sixty.

Farming in the mid-nineteenth century

IN the nineteenth century, just as in the fourteenth century, Aldsworth was at the very centre of the area that produced the finest Cotswold sheep. After the land was enclosed, more sheep than ever were kept. Roots were grown as winter fodder and the sheep 'folded' on it: that is, penned in to eat a small area of the crop at a time. (In the Middle Ages, the stewards of the monastic lands in Aldsworth had had to bring in hay as winter fodder for the sheep from their other estates nearby.) In the 1860s there were over 2,300 sheep in Aldsworth. In 1829 William Garne let rams for hire. From 1844 annual sheep sales were held at Blackpits. Sheep from Blackpits were exported to the USA by sailing ship in 1832. In 1849, 1850, 1851 and 1852 William Garne took first prizes for long-woolled sheep at the Royal Agricultural Society's show, held each year in a different part of the country. Railways had made this possible. The nearest station to Aldsworth was Fairford, until the line to Fossecross was built in 1851. Robert Garne continued the sheep sales until the end of the century and also showed sheep and won prizes.

Ladbarrow Farmhouse

Not as many cattle as sheep were kept in Aldsworth. They were the traditional long-horned variety, and long-horned oxen, or Hereford crosses, were used as draught animals. In the second half of the century shorthorn cattle began to replace the longhorns, and shire horses began to replace the oxen.

The coming of the railways meant that fertilisers such as guano could be brought to the countryside and used to increase crop yields. The improvement in transport must have helped rich and poor alike. Already before the railways came to Gloucestershire the roads had been greatly improved and the Severn Thames Canal system linking Gloucester and Bristol to Lechlade was completed in 1792, so heavy goods such as timber and coal could be more easily transported. Access to coal at affordable prices must have made a huge difference to the quality of life for ordinary people in this area, where finding enough wood to burn must always have been a problem. That is probably why the older cottages in the area are so small.

There was plenty of employment on the farms. The middle decades of the nineteenth century were a time of prosperity for the whole nation, for farming as well as for trade and industry. The population of Great Britain was growing and there was an ever-increasing demand for corn, meat and wool. Not until the 1870s and 1880s did it become possible to import large quantities of these products from Russia, the USA, Argentina, Australia and New Zealand by railway and steamship, from which time prices fell and fell.

In 1851 there were eighty-four men and boys employed in agriculture in Aldsworth. In 1871 there were eighty-three; in 1891 eighty-five. Farm wages until the mid-century at least must have been high enough to support a family, for the population of the village continued to rise. In 1851 it was 379; in 1861, 430. By 1871 it was 395.

Many farmhouses, such as Blackpits and Ladbarrow, and many large barns and other farm buildings were built or rebuilt at this time of agricultural prosperity. Some substantial houses for farm workers, such as New Row and Blackpits Farm cottages, were also built.

Trades and occupations

IN 1861, when the number of people living in Aldsworth reached its highest ever recorded level of 430, a large variety of goods and services was available in the village. There were two blacksmiths, three masons, four carpenters, one slatter and plasterer, two carriers, four shoemakers (of whom one was a 'master cordwainer'), one tailor, two dressmakers, one laundress, one cotton weaver, two bakers, three grocers and a rat catcher. There was a malthouse and brewery that also sold spirits.

Ninety-two men and boys worked on the land – six shepherds, three oxmen, nine carters, sixty-one agricultural labourers and thirteen ploughboys. Employed in domestic service were eight maidservants, two cooks and three nursemaids, and there were four grooms to private households. There were 158 children up to 14 years old. Ninety-seven of these were aged between 5 and 14, of whom only forty-one are listed as 'scholars' or schoolchildren. There was only one schoolteacher, Ann Collett, daughter of the blacksmith, aged 20. There were sixty-one children up to 4 years old.

In 1851 there was a cooper but none is recorded in later censuses. A trade directory of 1856 records two wheelwrights, but none is mentioned in the censuses of population from 1851 onwards.

Agricultural depression

B Y 1875 farm prices were falling fast as large quantities of grain were being imported from the USA and wool from the colonies.

In the years 1878–81 farmers were also hit by terrible weather. It was cold and wet. In 1879 the harvest was ruined; 1880 was nearly as bad.

In the 1890s the general agricultural depression deepened. Thousands of acres went out of cultivation – 2 million acres altogether nation-wide. Wages for farmworkers failed to rise and there was less work available. There were as many agricultural labourers as before, but they were less well off. They were underemployed, and were only paid for the days they worked.

When buildings decayed or farm cottages fell down there was no money to replace them. There are many examples in Aldsworth of single cottages being divided into two or three dwellings in the late nineteenth or early twentieth century. It was not until after the Second World War that housing conditions generally improved. In a survey of Gloucestershire published in 1939 by the County Council Planning Department, Aldsworth was included in the list of villages needing improved housing.

Progress in the early twentieth century

IN 1900 the Slatter family were farming the Rectory Manor Farm. Thomas Reginald Slatter and his wife Edith had four children, Sara, Lois, Owen and David, born between 1902 and 1913. In 1900 when Robert Garne died, his nephew W. T. Garne gave up the tenancy of Blackpits and Wall Farm and bought the house nearby that had belonged to the Tayler family, to which he added a new wing, a conservatory and a tennis court. He was the first in the village to have solid-fuel central heating, and an acetylene gas lighting plant. The first telephone in the village was installed in his house and he bought a motor car. The Slatter family also had a motorcar – a Cadillac, later replaced by a Ford. Petrol came in 2-gallon tins.

Few roads were tarred before the 1930s. They were just dressed with stones. Horse-drawn traffic and motorcars and steam engines did not co-exist very well. The horses would shy when they saw a car and the car-drivers would get shouted at; and when tarred surfaces suitable for cars were introduced they made the horses slip. Motorcars were only for the few. They were very expensive. In 1939 there were still only five in the village.

In 1925 when W. T. Garne died, his son Will, who had been living in Ablington, moved into his house with his wife and seven children, Helen, Susanna (Sue), Phyllis, William (Bill), Barbara, Pamela and Daphne. Transport was still mainly by horse and cart, or horse and trap or governess cart, and one could hire a carriage and pair. Sue Garne, born in 1910, remembers that her father disliked using the car. Once a week on a Monday he would go to market in Cirencester to sell his barley, and if any member of the family wished to go too, they went with him. The ostler at the King's Head Inn looked after the horse for 6d while they were in town. While their father was in the Corn Hall the other members of the family could do their shopping. But there was no need to carry everything home. Many firms, such as Gilletts the grocer, delivered to the village and the carrier's cart went from Aldsworth to Cirencester and back twice a week.

Sue Garne remembers learning to drive a car, which she was very reluctant to do. She was taught by Mr Crook of the Sherborne Arms. When she first drove her small sisters to school in Cirencester, she encountered a flock of sheep on the way, which she says took years off her life. It was usual in those days for herds of cattle and flocks of sheep to be driven along the main road.

Sue Garne remembers the very first bus in Aldsworth. Basil Howse built the chassis, and Rufus Harris did the bodywork. In 1929 the Garne family and some of the Tayler family took the bus for a family outing to Tidworth on Salisbury Plain to see the Military Tattoo. They stopped for a picnic in the New Forest. About twenty were in the party including Sue, Phyllis and their brother Billy, and Arthur Garne, whose mother was a daughter of the Tayler family who ran the brewery in Aldsworth. From this beginning Basil Howse built up a very successful bus business in the 1930s based on the yard that is now called Ashdale Close. Passengers were taken from Aldsworth and the neighbouring villages of The Barringtons, Windrush, Sherborne and Northleach to and from Cirencester and Cheltenham.

In 1920 a piped water supply was brought to the village from Windrush. Previously all water had been drawn from wells. Now every house had a tap. But inside flush lavatories and bathrooms did not always follow straightaway. There were still quite a few cottages without these amenities in the 1980s.

Mains electricity did not come to the village until the 1940s. Until it did, oil lamps and candles were used for lighting.

Farming in the early twentieth century

THE 210 acres of Green Farm were sold in 1897. The land and house were bought by W. T. Garne. In 1900 Mr Tom Rich from Cornwall took over the tenancy of Blackpits from W. T. Garne; and the Jefferies family from Cirencester took over Wall Farm at about the same time. From about 1890 the tenant of the Rectory Manor Farm was George Reginald Slatter. By 1891 Henry Lane had taken over at Cocklebarrow from his father William, who had been there since the middle of the century. At Ladbarrow the Houltons were succeeded by George Hewer, and he in 1912 by Tom Garne.

The agricultural depression of the late nineteenth century lasted until the First World War. With war trade was disrupted and food became scarce. Agricultural committees with emergency powers were set up to encourage an increase in production of cereals and meat. Farming became profitable again. The price of wheat rose from £9 to £17 a ton during this time.

But most of the men had left the land to fight for their country. It was left to old men, young boys and women to do all the work on the farms. Thirteen of the men lost their lives in the service of their country and are commemorated in the church, and on the war memorial erected on the village green after the war. Others survived but did not return to the village.

Some farms in the days before tractors had steam engines. Owen Slatter, born in 1906, who lived at the Manor as a boy until 1919, remembers that there was one on the farm there. Tom Sidford, who was in charge of it, called it his 'Blackbird'. It was a mobile steam engine, which could be used for various tasks.

In 1919 Reginald Slatter retired from farming and the A'bear family from Berkshire took over the Manor Farm, where they stayed until the 1970s. From 1914 to 1918 John Phillips (also known as S. J. Phillips) and his wife farmed Cocklebarrow. Arthur Garne took over the tenancy of this farm from him.

Prosperity for farmers did not long outlast the war. In 1922 prices of farm products fell to half their previous level. The price of wheat dropped to £8 a ton in 1931. Many tenant farmers went out of business. In Aldsworth 740 acres went uncultivated in 1926. Landlords suffered too as rents fell.

The situation was so bad that Lord Sherborne could find no tenant at all for Blackpits Farm in the last years of the 1920s. When S. J. Phillips took it on in 1930 he had the land rent-free for a year. Some farmers carried on as before, sometimes restricted by clauses in their leases, but others, usually newcomers, tried new methods such as using more fertiliser, feeding animals scientifically, and introducing new types of seed and new breeds of sheep. Some turned to dairying and pig keeping.

Will Garne, who had been living in Ablington with his wife and family, took over from his father in 1925. He continued to farm the Green Farm land and his other properties in the traditional way, keeping the herd of pedigree shorthorn cattle and the flock of Cotswold sheep.

In 1933 Lord Sherborne sold Ladbarrow Farm with its 600 acres to Maurice Willes from Upper Slaughter, who came there at the age of 19. At that time there were nineteen carthorses and eighteen men on the farm, and farming here too was carried out in the traditional way. After harvest, one day would be spent threshing and loading, and the next day the horse-drawn wagons (of the sort that would now be in an agricultural museum) would set off at 5 a.m. for Shipton-under-Wychwood, 12 miles away, returning in the afternoon, and this two-day cycle would be repeated.

Arthur Garne at Cocklebarrow introduced a dairy herd and delivered milk daily to Eastington and Northleach.

Sports and pastimes, 1900 to the 1950s

THERE was a cricket team in Aldsworth in the early twentieth century. The pitch was to the right of the road to Ladbarrow, on land that was then part of Manor Farm.

The A'bear family, with seven sons, could supply a large part of a team themselves. Matches were played against teams in neighbouring villages. In the 1930s young Maurice Willes was captain. Every year the team played a 'needle-match' against Upper Slaughter, his parents' village.

There was also a football team, which played matches with other teams in the area. The pitch was in the field where the Village Hall now stands. Six-a-side football was still played there in the 1980s. As for rugby football, there was no team in the village, but later, in the 1950s, Ken Taylor was a fine player who played for Gloucester. It is said that he could have played for Scotland had he not been so dedicated to his job and his family.

Darts was played in the pub and there were village teams that competed with teams from other villages. Dominoes and cribbage were also played.

For the gentry and wealthy farmers, foxhunting was the favourite sport. Besides keeping foxes under control it provided an opportunity for farmers to meet their neighbours and to get to know every inch of their own and their neighbours' land. When there was a meet in the village, many people would turn out to see the hounds, the huntsmen in their red coats and the elegantly attired mounted followers and many would follow on foot.

For the upper classes there were also pheasant and partridge shoots. Many people in the village could earn a little extra by acting as beaters or opening gates for huntsmen. When the pheasant season was over, nearly every farmer would organise a hare-shoot on his land. Everyone in the village with a gun would be invited to bring it along and an army of beaters was assembled. It was quite usual for 500–600 hares to be bagged in one day.

At harvest time the rabbits in the corn would gradually get penned into the middle of the field being reaped. Then all the village people would come with sticks to finish them off. This hardly counts as sport, but it certainly was a good way of getting an extra meat meal, and was particularly appreciated in wartime when food was scarce.

Several people in the village kept ferrets for catching rabbits.

In some reminiscences of Arthur Garne, written down towards the end of his life, he describes Aldsworth Feast (pronounced 'fiyast') which went on for a week at the time of St Bartholomew's Day in August. Aldsworth Band paraded for the church service, headed by someone carrying the two little flags that were kept in the church and the drum that was kept in Chapel Row. There were roundabouts pulled by ponies or mules and all the fun of the fair on the bit of ground in front of School House – after which, one gathers, everyone got very drunk and didn't go back to work for a week! The time he was writing about was the very beginning of the twentieth century, but this sounds like the relic of an old traditional feast, recorded in 1785, and one indirectly referred to by the disapproving vicar in his report of 1859. It is interesting that the area in front of the former pub was still used for the fun fair after the pub had gone.

When there was no radio or television, people had to make their own entertainment. Ted A'bear, who came to the village in 1919 at the age of 10, remembers the concerts which were given at the school at that time. Basil Howse was a talented performer as was the schoolmaster, Mr Robinson. Ted A'bear remembers John Stevens' son Reg singing songs and telling stories when the A'bear sons worked together with him in the fields, weeding, hoeing and charlock pulling; and he remembers Jimmy Midwinter, brother of John, who worked at Manor Farm, playing a tin-whistle.

There were dances and whist drives too, held at the school, and there was storytelling and singing down at the pub.

In the 1920s and 1930s a church fête was held in the summer on a site near the vicarage and later on the same site as the cricket pitch. There was a big tent with a show of produce and prizes for various classes of cakes, flowers, fruit and vegetables, and for flower arrangements, including some of wild flowers and grasses. There were competitions for children, merry-go-rounds and coconut shies. The day ended with a six-a-side football match.

Great national events were celebrated by large parties, which included the whole village. The earliest recollected was held in the Garnes' malthouse barn to celebrate the coronation of King George VI in 1937, though there must have been others before. The coronation of Queen Elizabeth II in 1953 was celebrated in Howse's Barn.

Everyone knew everyone else in the village and many were related to each other. With so few motorcars around it was safe for children to play outside. A favourite place to go was a little sloping pasture on the far side of the main road, opposite School House. It was described as being edged on the roadside by a bank so that the children were invisible to people in the village. Old photographs show two banks 20–30 feet long with paths around and between them, obviously leading up to the downs. Is it possible that here were a couple of the ancient burial mounds called barrows? We shall never know because these interesting features of the landscape were lost in a road-widening scheme when the contours of the land were altered to improve visibility along the road.

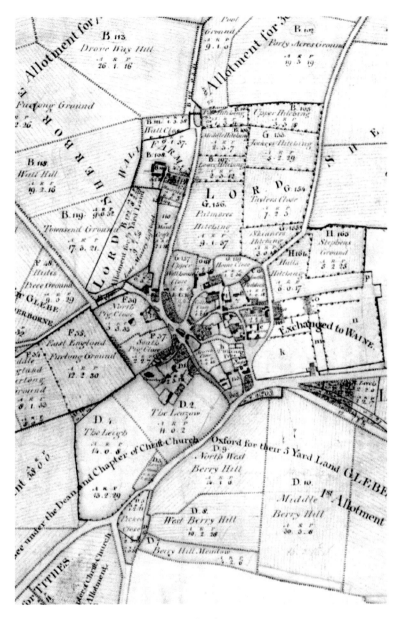

1. Aldsworth Enclosure Map, 1799 – detail

2. John 'Crump' Dutton, 1594–1657　　*3. Sir Ralph Dutton, Bt, 1642/3–1721*

4. Sir John Dutton, Bt, 1682–1743　　*5. James Lenox Naper Dutton,*
1712–1776

6. *Scene at Bibury Club race meeting, 1801. The Prince of Wales is the third mounted figure from the left.*

7. *'The Barracks', Wall Farm (distance), Pear Tree Cottages (centre)*

8. Gravestones in the churchyard

9. Gravestones in the churchyard

10. The former school, 2001

11. The Old School House, 2001

12. Green Farm House, 2001

13. Howard's Barn, now Windrush House, 2001

14. View of Green Farm from the Cirencester–Burford road, 2001

15. Howard's Cottage, 2001

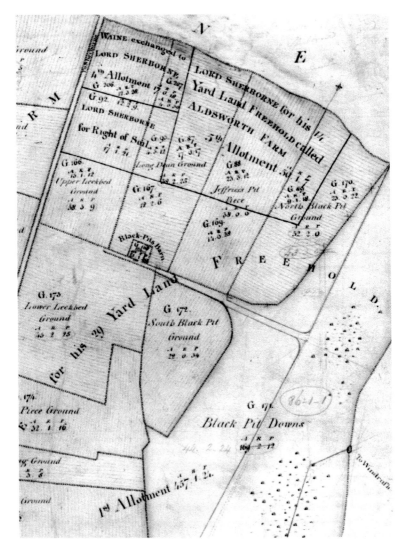

16. *Aldsworth Enclosure Map, 1799 – detail*

Life in the village, 1920–50

NEARLY all the cottages in the village had gardens and there were also allotments on the corner between the roads to Burford and to Ladbarrow, and opposite the vicarage. People in the village grew their own vegetables and fruit and were skilled gardeners. Some kept poultry or a pig or two. Some had beehives. There were also smallholders farming in the middle of the village itself. Rufus Harris, who lived opposite the forge and was also an undertaker and carpenter, kept a couple of cows on some land by the road to Ladbarrow, and milked them and made butter in a shed behind the house. He delivered milk from a churn with a ladle round the village. Joey Howard, living in the house now called Howard's Cottage, had the paddock and barn opposite his house, and some grazing land behind the Barracks. He kept pigs, cows and poultry for many years until he died in 1951 aged 88.

Bread formed a large part of the diet, and the bakery run by Charlie Legg was a focal point of the village. It sold buns and lardy cake too. The women at home made jam and

The Old Bakery

chutney and bottled fruit and vegetables, especially pickled onions. Some in the village made wine from cowslips, parsnips, hawthorn berries, rhubarb or other fruit; oranges, lemons and sugar were often also ingredients. The pigs raised were slaughtered in the village and turned into faggots, chitterlings, lard (which was flavoured with rosemary), sausages and bacon in people's homes.

Many households relied on an open fire for cooking and heating.

In those days, before the introduction of washing machines, spin driers and modern washing powder, the women performed heroic feats to get the washing done.

There were several shops in the village then, though there are none now. The busiest was Mrs Salvage's next to the school, which sold groceries and general provisions. The Post Office near the main road sold a few items such as biscuits, sweets and cigarettes.

Mr Legg the baker delivered bread and Mr Harris milk. Castles the butchers of Northleach delivered meat. Gilletts of Cirencester and Hornes of Northleach delivered groceries. Garne's Brewery of Burford called once a fortnight to deliver beer to private houses as well as the pub. Coal was, of course, delivered, and a van selling paraffin and hardware called on Thursdays.

People had their own remedies for ailments – a teaspoonful of brimstone and treacle, or syrup of figs for the children once a week; or honey for wounds. But the doctor from Burford would call on anyone who was ill, and the district nurse did her rounds on a bicycle. The doctor would call in the village to enquire about patients and leave prescribed medicines at the Reading Room – just as in the 1970s and 1980s, Dr Sharpley would call on Mrs Crewe at the Post Office for information, and leave medicines there.

Not many houses had bathrooms but people kept clean, often having a bath once a week in a tub in front of the fire.

Apart from farming, the major source of employment in the village at this time was the transport business run by

Basil Howse and his son Cyril. About a dozen people were employed in the 1930s and 1940s, driving and maintaining the buses and lorries, and quite a few of them lived in Aldsworth. Having a bus company on the doorstep must have been very liberating for inhabitants of this isolated village. Now a group of them – whether a darts team or a party of schoolchildren – could go together on a trip to a neighbouring village or town, which would have been impossible in the days of horse-drawn transport.

The school, 1920–79

KEN Stevens recalls that there were ninety pupils at the school when he was there from 1929 to 1938. They walked to school from nearby, but also from Swyre Farm (one from a gamekeeper's cottage near Dean Farm), Ladbarrow, Cocklebarrow, Kilkenny and Broadfield – for some a distance of several miles each way. They brought their lunch with them. Arthur Garne, who lived at Cocklebarrow from 1918, remembers fifty-two children coming past his house on their way to school. Few had watches or reliable clocks at home, so on some days they would arrive too early and others late.

Among the headteachers of the school were

Mr Robinson	from before 1919
Mr Crittington	1930s
Mr Bevin	1930s
Miss Browning	1940s and 1950s
Mr Harber	1960s to 1979

There were three classes in the school. The headteacher took the senior class. Teachers of the junior pupils were Miss Kitchen, Miss Price, Miss Sparrow, Miss Nelms and Miss Downing. Two of the teachers married sons of the A'bear family at Manor Farm. Miss Nelms married Fred A'bear and Miss Downing married Charlie A'bear.

The village green was the children's playground, where they played football and traditional games with tops and marbles. There was a garden behind the school where the boys grew vegetables. A woodwork shed, on the site of the present church car park, was unfortunately burnt down in the 1930s.

During the war the number of pupils in the school went up to well over a hundred because some forty children came to Aldsworth as evacuees from London. Extra classes were set up in the Methodist Chapel. Two extra teachers came too and were lodged in the vicarage.

After the 1939–45 war the number of pupils in the school fell. In 1979 there were only nineteen children on the school roll, and not all of them were from Aldsworth. The school closed in that year. Now the children of Aldsworth go by bus or car to Bibury Church of England Primary School, and then to Farmors School, Fairford, or the Cotswold School at Bourton-on-the-Water.

In 1999 a school reunion of Aldsworth Church of England School's former pupils was held in the new Village Hall and many attended, including many of the evacuees, who have happy memories of their wartime school days.

The Second World War, 1939–45

LIKE villages up and down England, Aldsworth was prepared for a German invasion at the beginning of the war. Every road sign and railway sign was removed to confuse German spies. No church bells were rung during the war, as the ringing of the bells was to be the signal that the Germans had landed. A Home Guard of fifteen men and boys was formed. Jim Ind was Sergeant-Major. There were no uniforms, and the first weapons were brooms, since there were not enough rifles to go round. A big elm-tree trunk was placed at the entrance to the village by School House, one end fixed to a pivot and the other to a wheel so that it could be wheeled across to block the road. This was done every night, and a candle in a jam-jar was positioned to show that it was there, as it could not be seen in the blackout. One night when the candle was missing, the Sergeant-Major from Windrush drove into the barricade, for the black-out was total and even car headlights had shades.

Frank Simpson was in the Home Guard. He was 14 when he came to Aldsworth in 1939 from London, with his twin brother John and aunt Mrs Cordery, to stay with his grandmother, Mrs Simpson, in Church Lane. He had just left school and went to work at Blackpits Farm, the land of which lies next to Windrush Camp where there was an airfield. He remembers that when the Germans dropped firebombs on and around the airfield, the Home Guard went to put them out. While he was working in the fields he witnessed many incidents. He saw as many as fourteen planes piloted by inexperienced trainee pilots crash land in Blackpits' fields.

There were very many airfields in the sparsely populated and lightly wooded open countryside of east Gloucestershire and west Oxfordshire. Most were used for pilot training. The airfields for bombers were mainly in East Anglia, closer to Germany. The airfield nearest to Aldsworth was at Windrush Camp. Blackpits cover, a stand of beech trees running north from the Burford road, was felled because it was on the flight path, and was replanted when the war was over. Other airfields nearby were at Rissington, Fairford, Ablington, Chedworth, Southrop and Bradwell Grove. Rissington was particularly useful as it was in a fog-pocket at night and could not be located by German bombers.

Late in the evening of 18 August 1940, one of the hardest days of the Battle of Britain, Sergeant Bruce Hancock, a young trainee pilot, with others, was doing night practice at Windrush Airfield. A German Heinkel saw lights and attacked the airfield, dropping ten bombs. It then saw and

fired on Bruce Hancock's Avro Anson. Witnesses saw
Sergeant Hancock turn and deliberately ram the German
plane. The two planes crashed in Turrets field to the right of
the Aldsworth to Sherborne road. Jack Parrot and Fred Ind in
Aldsworth heard the sound of a bomb and rushed to the
scene. Fred Ind was guiding vehicles into the field with the
aid of his flashlamp when he was arrested and detained
overnight as a suspected German spy! The Heinkel exploded
and burst into flames. The five Germans in it and Bruce
Hancock were all killed. The remains of the planes were dug
up in the mid-1970s and the families of the airmen contacted.
A plaque commemorating the incident was dedicated and
fixed on the wall in Windrush Church in 1988. A similar
plaque was placed on the control tower of Windrush Airfield.

Another dramatic incident involved a Mosquito that came
over Wall Farm with one engine burning, hit the chicken
shed, killing some chickens, collided with some cows, killing
six, and then crashed in a field on the far side of the
Sherborne road. By that time the fire was longer burning.
When the Home Guard reached the scene, the two airmen
had got out and were sitting on a bank smoking a fag!

Frank Simpson remembers once being at Kilkenny Valley
Ground in a field of barley with a horse and cart and wagon
when a German plane flew low along the valley on its way to
bomb the Hurricane planes at Ablington. The horses bolted,
but the men stood their ground and found themselves
looking directly into the eyes of the pilot. The plane reached
Ablington and the crew shot and killed some British airmen.
It was then chased by British aircraft all the way to
Portsmouth and shot down.

A wing fell off a training plane and fell into a yard of
cattle at Stone Barn Blackpits, a mile from the village. At
Ladbarrow a plane crashed into one of the electricity pylons,
killing one of the crew.

On moonlit nights, sitting outside Green Farmhouse on
the bench now called Coronation Bench, Frank Simpson
remembers seeing hundreds of German bombers overhead

going to bomb Bristol and Coventry. Many people in the Cotswolds area recall seeing the glow in the sky from the burning city of Coventry.

Lodge Park and Sherborne House were requisitioned and occupied by American troops. Sherborne Park was used to train troops for D-Day. Heaps of bombs were stacked along the road from Aldsworth to Bibury; Chedworth woods were also full of bombs.

In the build-up to D-Day, American tanks came along the road night and day from Cirencester past Aldsworth on their way to the A40. There were so many that some were stuck for half a day in the village before they moved.

Many inhabitants of the village served in the forces during the war. Some lost their lives; all are listed in Appendix D.

Life in wartime

FRANK Simpson remembers that at the beginning of the war the main entertainment was playing darts in the pub, which was run by Mr Crook. The beer came in jugs and the pub was lit by oil lamps. Electricity did not come to Aldsworth until towards the end of the war. As the war progressed, beer became in short supply. Sometimes one would order a pint of beer and get a pint of milk instead! Cigarettes were also hard to come by. One had to be on good terms with the Misses Haines behind the counter at the Post Office to get any.

Food was rationed; cheese, onions and very fat bacon were a large part of the diet. Some people kept chickens and rabbits. Every household kept a pig or two. All farms had to grow potatoes and there were allotments as well as people's gardens for growing vegetables. Everyone was encouraged to 'Dig for Victory'.

London was heavily bombed at the beginning of the war, so children were evacuated to country areas to escape the

'Blitz'. Forty came to Aldsworth and were taken into households in the village. Extra classrooms were set up in the Methodist Chapel. Many of the evacuees still visit Aldsworth years later.

During the war, dances were held every Saturday night at the school. Aldsworth had its own band, which included 'Marnie Legg', the baker's daughter. There were also whist drives at the school. Dances were also held at Barrington Village Hall.

Not many people had cars in the 1940s, and petrol was rationed, but there was a good bus service, and departures were timed so that one could go to 'the pictures' or out for the evening in Cheltenham or Cirencester. There were also bicycles, which, as the roads were uncrowded, could be safely used to get from one village to another. If one did have a car, the petrol pump outside the pub was useful. Shopping was not a problem as there were many delivery services.

When Victory in Europe Day and Victory in Japan Day came, many were still far from home. Fifty years on, in 1995, there was more time to reflect. A beacon was lit on Berry Hill as part of the nation-wide celebrations, and the site of the new Village Hall was dedicated. Many people then told of wartime experiences they had never communicated to anyone before, either through lack of opportunity or because they had been sworn to secrecy.

Farming, 1939–2000

FRANK Simpson, an evacuee, came to work at Blackpits Farm in 1939 at the age of 14. He came from Southwark, East London, and his memories are vivid. He worked with the fourteen carthorses, most of which were black and white shires. Gregory Phillips bred his own and they were on the farm until the end of the war. The carters' day started at 5 a.m., since the horses had to be harnessed before work could begin. First they had to be caught, having been turned out in the 'Hitching' the night before. Sometimes the men could not catch them at all! At Manor Farm the carter's name was William Kite and he lived at the Manor Lodge. The Manor Farm carthorses were turned out in the paddock across the road: it was called 'Pimlico Dock'.

Ken Stevens, born in 1924, grew up in the first cottage on the drive up to Swyre Farm, where his father was cowman. When he left school in 1939 he went to work at Manor Farm, where he drove one of the first tractors. It had no mudguards and the wheels came round past his ears. It was very mucky, and dusty in the summer. His call-up papers came but his employer refused to let him leave – so he found another job. As soon as he was able, he left to join the Royal Navy, although he was in a reserved occupation. After the war he worked as a lorry driver for C. J. Howse.

Frank Simpson remembers taking a horse and cart down School Lane to fetch water from the Fair well for the sheep. It was steep and rutted.

There was only one tractor at Blackpits in 1939. It drove the threshing machine. The first combine harvester came from America through the lend-lease system. There was a combine trailer and a lend-lease tractor to pull it. An old bus was cut down to make a flat-bed lorry to take the corn as it came out of the hopper on the combine. It then had to be shovelled into sacks in the barn. German prisoners of war did this work. Five of them came every day from Birdlip with a guard.

Frank Simpson recalls that there were sixteen farmworkers at Blackpits. Among them were Will, Jack and Ray Parrot; George, Frank and Ernie Howell; George Kite; Jack Curly; Fred and Jim Ind; George Paish; Walter Iles; Petty the shepherd; and Forsyth the cowman. Young women were conscripted to work on the land during the war, and two sisters, May and Ellen, were sent to Aldsworth from London. May later married Jack Parrot.

At Wall Farm the Wilcox family, who took over the tenancy in 1940, brought a dairy herd of thirty-six shorthorn

Blackpits Farm House

cows with them. The Milk Boards had already been
established. The milk went in 10-gallon and 13-gallon churns
by Bedford lorry to the CWS Co-op at Latton. By 1945 there
was a milking machine run by a Lister engine. When dairying
started up again in 1975 after a seven-year interval, Friesian
cows replaced the shorthorns and milk was transported by
tanker. From 1940 the Wilcoxes kept pigs – saddlebacks
crossed with a large white boar. They were sold to the firm of
Gilletts, which had a bacon factory in Cirencester.

Arthur Garne had a dairy herd in the 1940s and 1950s and
delivered milk to houses nearby. He later kept saddleback
pigs and poultry. Reg Pinchin at the Old Forge had a bottling
plant. Rufus Harris and Joey Howard in the middle of the
village also kept a few cows and pigs.

Ken Taylor, later farm manager for Gregory Phillips,
remembers Blackpits Farm from 1953 when he came as a
lorry driver. Farm work then was back-breaking, mind-
numbing hard labour. All the grain had to be put into
4-bushel sacks. Each sack took $2\frac{1}{4}$ cwt of wheat, 2 cwt of
barley, or $1\frac{3}{4}$ cwt of oats (wheat being heavier than barley,
which is heavier than oats). A hundredweight, for which cwt is

an abbreviation, is 112 lbs, so the heaviest sacks weighed 252 lbs each. A sack would be pushed down a chute on to the back of each working man and then had to be loaded into the lorries. The sacks were called Gopsall Browns, and were fetched by the lorry-load from Gloucester. They served many purposes. In the days before heated cabs, or indeed any cabs at all, many a tractor driver would wrap a few Gopsall Browns around him to save him from freezing to death in the fields.

There were sheep and Hereford cattle at Blackpits in the 1940s and 1950s. Crops grown were wheat, barley, oats, mangolds, kale and potatoes. Every farm had to grow potatoes during the war and the authorities were very strict about this. Workers came from the Polish camp for displaced persons at Daglingworth to dig the potatoes. Local people dug potatoes too. Pay was 24s a day.

In 1951 the first grain drier came to Blackpits and the large barn was built to house it. Over the years ever larger and more efficient machinery was used. More fertiliser and more chemicals were used; yields increased greatly, land prices rose.

Horses were no longer needed and were gradually phased out. There had been about seventy working horses on the farms and not long after the war there were none. Mechanisation meant that fewer farm workers were needed. Whereas in 1938 between seventy and eighty men were employed on the farms, after the war that fell to about twenty. Pay and conditions improved for those who were still employed.

After the war, government controls and intervention payments saved farmers from the disastrous effects of sudden falls in market prices. A new kind of subsidy replaced this when the UK joined the European Common Market and the Common Agricultural Policy. New crops such as oilseed-rape and linseed have appeared in the fields. Fields of oats are almost never seen, as there are no working horses to feed, and few if any potatoes are grown.

Farming in the post-war period prospered. Only in the last few years of the millennium was it in crisis again.

Will Garne at Green Farm

F ROM 1925 until 1967, in the midst of all the changes being
made around him, Will Garne at Green Farm, right in the
middle of the village, carried on farming in the same way as
his father and great uncle had done before, keeping his herd
of pedigree shorthorn cattle, which were housed in the barn
and sheds opposite the present Post Office, and the flock of
Cotswold sheep which had been in the family for so long.

Born in 1880, Will had been brought up at a time when
the family fortunes were at their peak, always having the
best of everything. In 1906 he had married Frances Minchin,
then aged 22, daughter of a neighbouring farming family,
and judging by photographs taken at the time of their
marriage he and his wife made a very handsome couple. At
Hinton Farm in Ablington, bought by his great-uncle Robert,
he and his wife enjoyed an idyllic early married life. Will
enjoyed hunting and shooting and his wife produced seven
children. When his father died in 1925 the family moved into
the house in Aldsworth. Although the fortune inherited by
W. T. Garne from his uncle Robert had dwindled somewhat,
and was now shared between his three children, the family
was still wealthy. Will's share was the house and Green
Farm. The Garne name was known in farming circles all over
England for their success in breeding prize-winning stock. At
the age of 45 Will Garne saw no reason not to carry on as
before and continue the pleasant lifestyle to which he was
accustomed.

His father had made the great transition from being a
tenant farmer to owning his own house and land. As a result,
during the terrible slump of the 1920s and 1930s, Will Garne
and his family were unfettered by the restrictions of a lease
and were able to continue living as before, enjoying hunting,
tennis parties, picnics and many social events, in the house
that had never had a name but is now known as Taylers
Farmhouse. Then and later they were able to carry on by

cutting down on maintenance and selling assets as necessary. Will never had the ultimate incentive to change which so many farmers had to face during those difficult times: that of threatened or actual bankruptcy.

He himself was an acknowledged expert and judge of shorthorn cattle. Good beef bulls were still in demand and he knew how to produce them, and he was ably assisted by his herdman Albert Forsyth. The Cotswold sheep were not very profitable but thrived in the care of their shepherd Jim Wilcox, who never married and devoted his whole life to their welfare until he died aged 81 in 1953. As a lucrative sideline Will bred prize-winning black red game cocks to show and sell as his father and great-uncle had done before.

Will continued hunting, which he had enjoyed since he was 10, until well past his eightieth birthday, never missing a meet if he could possibly help it. He maintained a Victorian attitude to his wife and daughters, not allowing them to take any part in the farming, although of course they were very busy running the house and garden, growing vegetables and fruit and keeping poultry.

At the beginning of the Second World War, Will was nearly 60. His only son Bill left home in 1939 at the age of 24 when his regiment, the Wiltshire Yeomanry, was mobilised and he was posted abroad, so he was not at home to help his father during the war years. It is not surprising that Will gave up the tenancy of Swyre Farm rather than plough up grassland as farmers were required to do in wartime. He and his ageing workforce had no experience of mechanised arable farming, for which the Green Farm land was not suited. He bought another small farm for his son.

After the war he continued to be a partner in a firm that bought pedigree stock for export. He kept the shorthorn herd which now had the oldest pedigree of any in England. He refused even to think about giving up the flock of Cotswold sheep which were still cared for by Jim Wilcox, and after his death, with equal devotion, by his successor as shepherd, Jack Bond.

In the 1960s Will Garne's magnificent stand against change was rewarded when there was a revival of interest in old breeds. In 1966 the flock book for Cotswold sheep was restarted and he became President of the Cotswold Sheep Society. He died the following year aged 87.

The Cotswold breed was valued again not just for its history but for the qualities that had made it successful in the past. As well as producing good meat and wool, these sheep were large-framed, hardy, docile, long-lived and easy to lamb, with the ewes being good mothers. As the vast expanses of North America were opened up for agriculture in the nineteenth century, young Cotswold rams had been particularly in demand for crossing to improve other breeds and create new ones. Thousands of Cotswold sheep were exported into the USA from 1832 onwards. They were also exported to Canada, Australia, New Zealand, Germany, France, Austria and Russia. The best rams would fetch prices of 100 guineas or more. Right up to the start of the First World War foreign buyers would come to England to buy sheep from the most famous of the Cotswold flocks, such as that of the Garnes in Aldsworth and their rivals the Lanes of Broadfield Farm in Northleach. Often the buyers would stay in the farmhouse with the farmer and his family for days or even weeks. Ram lambs were sold for cross-breeding in England until the 1950s. Cotswold sheep could be enormous. Many mature rams weighed over 4 cwt; a young sheep of 2 years or less sent to slaughter could weigh 2 cwt. Gradually other breeds came to be preferred for meat and wool.

Cotswold sheep are distinctive in appearance. The wool is kinked and at first grows in tight curls, later becoming very long and giving the animal a shaggy appearance. The wool on the head grows into a forelock hanging down between the eyes.

After Will Garne's death in 1967 a new single-storey was built for his wife and daughter. The rest of the property was sold. Four houses, as well as a large barn suitable for conversion, and a site for a house were sold, so soon there were newcomers in the village.

The age of Queen Elizabeth II

A T the end of the war, the evacuees and soldiers and airmen went home and the social horizons for inhabitants of the village shrank. The loss of some fifty jobs on the farms led to a deterioration in the quality of life for many ordinary people in Aldsworth, none the less devastating for being spread over a period of thirty years or so. Farm wages had not been high but they had been spent in the village, and when they went other jobs and services went too. The bakery and the shops closed. The forge, of course, closed when there were no longer any working horses left to shoe. There were fewer delivery services and fewer buses. When Basil Howse sold the bus company to Marchants Coaches, jobs as bus drivers were lost to the village. The population aged as few new young people were taken on to work on the farms. There were fewer children. Whereas in the 1940s there had been over a hundred pupils at the school, in 1979 there were nineteen. The school, which had been so important in the lives of so many, and to which the village had contributed, closed in that year. Then there was no longer anywhere to hold regular social events such as dances and whist drives – even if there had been anyone to organise them, or indeed anyone to go. The plans to build a village hall came to nothing, though in the 1980s there was still a Village Hall Bank Account with a few hundred pounds in it.

Things were not all bad though. Newcomers found a friendly village in beautiful surroundings far from the ugly urban sprawl and heavy traffic of so much of the rest of England. Social events were held in the 1970s and 1980s, some of them in the school building. The church had some very enjoyable sit-down harvest lunches there. The British Legion had a barbecue every year and a dinner at Christmas. Queen Elizabeth II's 1977 Silver Jubilee was celebrated with a big party for all in the big drier barn at Blackpits. A church fête was held in the same barn each summer in June. There

was no longer a flower show but there were the usual stalls
for cakes, jams, plants and garden produce, crafts and bottles;
and fancy dress competitions, games and pony rides for the
children. Peter Percy's poultry business at the Manor brought
jobs to the village. C. J. Howse still employed a few people,
driving and maintaining the lorries. Six new houses had been
built after the war by the Council and there were a few other
new houses too. Pay and conditions for those still on the
farms improved greatly. Above all, the village still had its
Post Office and its pub.

The last of the Duttons

IN 1982 Charles Dutton, 7th Baron Sherborne since 1949,
died. During the Second World War he had been a pilot
with the Air Transport Auxiliary. His wife also flew planes.
They lived at Lodge Park but had no children. The title
passed to an 82-year-old cousin with no heirs. When he died
three years later, the title became extinct. The estate, much
depleted by death duties, had been left to the National Trust
in 1982. Most of the remaining property in Aldsworth was
then sold by the National Trust, so the Wilcoxes at Wall Farm
and the Phillips at Blackpits were able to buy the freehold of
their farms, and various houses were sold. In 1970 Christ
Church sold the land of its estate in Aldsworth and then the
Manor House. The days when almost everyone was a tenant
on a large estate were over.

The Phillips family

FOR most of the last hundred years the Phillips family have
been a powerful presence in Aldsworth as landowners,
tenant farmers, employers, friends and neighbours. Samuel

THE PHILLIPS FAMILY

71

John Phillips (S. J. Phillips) came to Aldsworth just before the
First World War and lived and farmed at Cocklebarrow with
his newly-wed wife from 1914 to 1918. These were the only
years he lived in the village, but during the 1930s he took
over many farms in or near the parish – Blackpits, Woeful
Lake, Kilkenny and Bibury. Over the years he and his sons
built up the huge agricultural business S. J. Phillips & Sons
(Kemble) Ltd, farming thousands of acres of Gloucestershire.

John Phillips' elder son Gregory (1918–97) was born at
Cocklebarrow. When he left school he came to Aldsworth to
live with Will Garne and family and learn about farming. In
1938 he took over Blackpits. After the war Gregory and his
wife Helen moved into Blackpits House, where they lived for
more than fifty years.

The story of S. J. Phillips as told by his wife Ruth in *Short
Story of a Farmer* is a fascinating one. His grandparents,
Richard Lawry and his wife, had been farming in Cornwall,
where rents were high, and had heard of good opportunities
for farmers in Gloucestershire. In 1891 the whole family
moved to Macaroni Downs – a small and isolated farm in the
parish of Eastleach 2 miles south-east of Aldsworth – with
their cattle and farm equipment. With Mr and Mrs Lawry
came two grown-up sons and two grown-up daughters, one
of whom was married to Samuel Phillips and had three small
children of 4 and 3 years. John was one of the 4-year-old
twins. The family were devout Methodists and attended the
chapel at Lechlade. John's farming career started just before
his fifteenth birthday when his grandfather died and he took
over Macaroni Farm where the family then lived (Macaroni
Downs being managed by his uncle). John's mother had died
when he was small and his father had returned to Cornwall.

John married Ruth Shawyer, daughter of the Mayor of
Swindon, in 1914 and the couple went to live at
Cocklebarrow Farm, Aldsworth, until 1918. The first three of
their six children were born there. John and his wife then
moved to Ewen Farm near Cirencester, and then took over
farms at Kemble. It was in Kemble that he and his wife made

their home, living for twenty-five years at 'The Limes'. Later, in 1950, he bought the Kemble Estate from Lord Biddulph and rebuilt Kemble House.

In 1930 John Phillips took the tenancy of Blackpits Farm, Aldsworth. For the first year it was rent-free and later the rent was from 2s 6d to 7s 6d an acre. In an era of agricultural depression when many tenant farmers were failing, this remarkable man could see possibilities for farming where others could not.

He also farmed Far Hill and Hook Farm, Fairford; Macaroni Farm; Kilkenny and Bibury Farms, Woeful Lake; and Trewsbury and Trull. During the Second World War he farmed Tarlton Farm; and Coates Farm for the Royal Agricultural College.

One of John Phillips' major talents was his ability to get on with people from all walks of life, and in particular his ability to choose and train good farm managers. Ted A'bear helped to manage the farms at Kemble in the 1930s and 1940s, and during the war when S. J.'s sons Gregory and Gordon were away on military service, he moved into the Phillips' house, 'The Limes'. Later he managed Kilkenny Farm. He remembers his employer as a clever, observant man, a successful farmer and a good boss, liked by all save a few who were jealous of him, and on equally easy terms with Earl Bathurst or the Duke of Beaufort as with a dustman.

S. J. Phillips' knowledge of farming in Gloucestershire was unsurpassed. He served on numerous committees, such as the Milk Board, the County Wages Board and the Small Holdings Board, and became Chairman of the National Union of Farmers several times. He was a member of the Parish Council, the District Council and the County Council, and sat on the magistrates' bench. His influence thus extended to the whole county of Gloucestershire, and beyond that to the whole country. He died in 1965 a very well-known and respected figure.

John's son Gregory took over Blackpits in 1938 but left soon afterwards to serve his country in the armed forces. In

1941 he was set ashore on the coast of Italy from a submarine to perform a special mission, which he accomplished; but unfortunately he was not picked up afterwards at the appointed rendezvous. He was captured, and from 1941 to 1945 he was held prisoner-of-war in Italy. In later life he would relate that he used the time to become an expert bridge player.

When Gregory returned from the war he married, in 1946, Helen Wakefield, whose family farmed near Burford, and they moved into Blackpits House. Their three children, Carol, John and Lavinia, were brought up there.

Gregory and Helen rode to hounds, owned racehorses, went shooting and deer stalking, and played tennis, golf and bridge. For seven years Gregory was Master of the Vale of White Horse FoxHounds. All this is remarkable because shortly before his marriage Gregory lost his right arm in a motor accident. It is a tribute to his determination and his wife's tender loving care that one was scarcely aware of his disability in his presence.

The Phillips were very sociable. It was typical of them that to celebrate their golden wedding they gave two enormous parties in a marquee outside the house for all their relations, friends, neighbours and employees, past and present.

During the half-century after the Second World War, a time of great prosperity for farming, the Phillips were the major farmers and employers in Aldsworth, and together with the other major landowner living in the village, Maurice Willes of Ladbarrow, set the tone of the village. It is thanks to them that the village was such a pleasant place to live in during that time.

Gregory died in 1997 and Helen in 1999. Their passing truly marked the end of an era in Aldsworth.

Gregory and Helen's son John and his wife Priscilla (Cilla) live at Kilkenny Farm. Their daughters, Carol Farmar and Lavinia Rank, also live nearby with their husbands and families.

The last ten years

IN the last ten years of the millennium there were many more newcomers and it became hard to keep up with the changes as houses were bought and sold. With improvements in cars and roads it is no longer necessary for people to live near their work, so the newcomers have jobs and businesses in a wide area around the village. There were some new houses at Manor Barn and Ashdale Close. The population became younger and there were more children. Young people were taken on again on the farms and they had children too.

The Village Hall

In 1995 the Village Hall Project was started and a committee formed. Land was donated by the Phillips family, and the architect Michael Cooper and solicitor Andrew Congreve gave their services free, as did the organisers. Much work went into fund-raising, particularly by Patsy Dawson and John O'Keeffe. Jane Murray and Rob Askew set up the excellent Heritage Room. The new National Lottery Fund gave money, as did other organisations and charities. Many in the village gave donations or helped to raise funds. The Village Hall was built on time and the result was very pleasing. On 9 September 1999 it was officially opened by Her Royal Highness Princess Anne, the Princess Royal. The

local schoolchildren greeted the Princess outside the Hall
when she arrived. Inside the Hall she was met by the Lord
Lieutenant of the County and local government officers
wearing their chains of office. The Lord Lieutenant
introduced the Princess to many of the large number of
inhabitants of the village who were assembled there, and the
Princess made a thoughtful impromptu speech.

On 31 December 1999 a large party was held to celebrate
the dawn of a new millennium. Thus ends a thousand years
in the history of Aldsworth, a village remarkable as much for
the ways in which it has not changed as for the ways in
which it has.

PART II

The Old Playground

THE lower of the two greens in Aldsworth is called 'The Old Playground' by some inhabitants of the village because that is what it was in their youth. The early village grew up around this green in the centuries before 1066 because here there was a reliable water supply. The Fair Well, recorded by that name in 1638, now sometimes called the Fairy Well, still provides a constant supply of clear spring water emerging from just below ground level. Before 1800 there were also several ponds here.

In the field that slopes up between the lane to the church and the house called 'The Barracks' there are the remains of old buildings in the form of clearly visible bumps in the grass. This must be the site of 'Aldsworth Farm House', mentioned in the Enclosure Act as being to the north-west of the church. The Enclosure Act described 'Aldsworth Farm' itself as 'belonging' to Lord Sherborne and as being 'heretofore part of the possessions of the dissolved Abbey of St Peter's in Gloucester'. Thus it seems clear that this site was the headquarters of the largest estate in the village. It had probably been so from the start. However, it is a curious fact that until 1793 this 7-acre plot was part of the Rectory Manor Estate associated with the church. This is made plain by a map of 1793 in Christ Church Library, Oxford.

The reason that the main farmhouse of the Aldsworth Farm Estate was not actually on the estate itself can probably best be explained thus. The 11 hides of land granted to St Peter's of Gloucester were in the north-east and north-west of the parish, where there is no surface water. Down the middle of the parish runs an underground water course that emerges here and there as springs or ponds – but the convenient sites along this were already occupied when St Peter's received its grant of land some time between 1008 and 1066. There had been a settlement at Wall Farm from time immemorial; and to the south Bibury Church had been an established presence for two or possibly three centuries, having the right to collect tithes and an estate of several hundred acres around its dependent chapel, which later

The Barracks

became St Bartholomew's Church. For the monks of St Peters it was so important to have a site with access to water – the spring for the humans and the ponds for the oxen, cows and other animals – that they were prepared to become tenants on the smaller estate. It appears from the wording of the Enclosure Act that the rent for this plot of land was £5 a year, and that in return the tenant of Aldsworth Farm received a bull and a boar from the rectory estate. This 'custom' or agreement was abolished by the Act.

Before 1793 the green would have looked quite different from how it does today. Besides the farmhouse and farm buildings on the slope behind, with the ponds below, there were six cottages on the green itself. Three of them (in one building) belonged to the churchwardens and may have been used to house the poor. They have gone now, but two of the gardens remain and the rent for them is still paid to the church. The changes to the green were made after 1793 so that Lord Sherborne could complete his carriageway from Sherborne House past Wall Farm and along in front of the Rectory Manor House to the main road. The largest pond, which was by the Fair Well, was in the way. So it was probably at this time that the ditch down the middle of the green was dug in order to drain it. The ditch is clearly not a natural feature. It and its bridge replaced a lane between the cottages, which had to be demolished.

'Aldsworth Farm House' and its farm buildings were now redundant. The site was now owned by Lord Sherborne, who had exchanged 29 acres of land in front of the Manor for it. It was enclosed with a wall and turned into 'Pig Close'. The role of principal farmhouse of the Aldsworth Estate was taken over by new farms at Cocklebarrow and Blackpits. By this time the technology of sinking wells and drawing or pumping water from them had greatly improved. It was no longer essential for a farm to be near a pond. A farmhouse and farm buildings were also built at Ladbarrow at about this time.

The house called 'The Barracks' appears to date from the eighteenth century. It may stand on the site of an earlier farm building or even the farmhouse itself. The name 'The Barracks' probably dates from the late eighteenth or early nineteenth century (see Appendix B). In the mid-nineteenth century, 'The Barracks' was converted to three cottages. In the 1920s, 1930s and 1940s these were occupied by the Edginton, Paish and Carter families. George Stevens lived in a cottage at the back. 'The Barracks' was sold by Lord Sherborne in 1976 and was converted to one house and a cottage. The house is said to be haunted.

A pair of semi-detached cottages that are part of Wall Farm – 'Pear Tree Cottages' – date from the nineteenth century. In 1799 there were two other cottages there. The tenant of one was Mary Waine. The tenant of the other was William Peacey, who was also tenant of about an acre nearby called 'Townsend Little Ground'. It is likely that this site, situated at the bottom of the present drive to Wall Farm, was once a vineyard, because at the time of the enclosure William Peacey exchanged a 17-acre site near Conygree with Lord Sherborne for 'Vineyard Close'. In the early Middle Ages, the climate in England was warm enough to grow grapes. At this time the only road to Wall Farm was the lane to the east.

At the opposite side of the green to 'The Barracks' was Well House, still there today. At the east end of the Old Playground is Bridge House, a small but attractive building. In the seventeenth and eighteenth centuries it belonged to the Mury family. Until some time in the late eighteenth century this freehold property included one yardland (approximately 30 acres). This was possibly the land in front of and to the south of the Manor, which in 1793 belonged to Lord Sherborne. A tablet on the front of the house is inscribed 'William Mury 1728'. In 1799 it belonged to John Tayler and was described as two messuages, shop garden and orchard. In 1841 it was acquired by the Revd John Bellingham, who in 1871 sold it to Christ Church. It was described at the time as a house and a shoemaker's shop. Recent occupants have been Mr and Mrs Wally Vincent and Mr and Mrs Clive Wharton and family.

The village pound used to stand where the former school now stands. It is shown on the 1799 enclosure map. Here stray animals were coralled until collected by their owners, on payment of a fine.

The former school is a fine stone building built in 1853. The school closed in 1979. A private nursery school was started in the building by Miss Fenella Palmer, and continued by Mrs Calcutt who bought the building from the National Trust, the heirs of Lord Sherborne. The building was sold for conversion to a private house in 1989. It was sold again and has been renamed Stonebury House.

The cottage on School Lane, no. 51, was occupied for most of the twentieth century by members of the Ind family. The lane here once led to a farmyard on the site of Blackpits Farmhouse.

The Church

S T BARTHOLOMEW'S Church stands on a hill above the lower of the two greens in Aldsworth, and is surrounded by an attractive churchyard, with interesting gravestones.

There was probably a church or chapel here in the ninth century. Anglo-Saxon England was converted to Christianity in the seventh century, and by 680 the Bishopric of Worcester had been established, maintained by the grant of estates throughout the diocese. One of these was leased in 725 to Earl Leppa and his daughter Beage, and became Bibury, where there was probably a church by AD 750. St Mary's Church, Bibury, became a minster church – a cross between a monastery and a mini-cathedral with a missionary function. Three dependent chapels in Winson, Barnsley and Aldsworth were set up. The 3 hides of land held by a priest in Bibury in 1086 have been identified as the later 'Rectory Manor of Bibury and Aldsworth'. There is no trace now of an Anglo-Saxon church in Aldsworth. Perhaps it was made of wood.

In 1151 Bibury Church and its properties were
'appropriated' – that is, taken over – by Oseney Abbey in
Oxford. It thus went outside the jurisdiction of the Diocese of
Worcester or of Gloucester, until the nineteenth century. It
was known as 'Bibury Peculiar' and had its own consistory
court, which dealt with wills, attendance at church services,
payment of debts and tithes, and moral transgressions.

The bishop of Worcester, however, in 1151, reserved the
right to appoint one canon to Oseney to undertake care of
souls in Bibury and to reside in the parish.

After the dissolution of the monasteries, Oseney Abbey's
property was granted to Christ Church, Oxford. So from 1546
the Dean and Chapter held the 'impropriate rectory', as it
was called: they also held the advowson – that is, the right to
appoint the vicar. They still had the latter in the 1980s, even
though their property in Aldsworth had been sold.

The earliest part of the present church is the Norman
north aisle, which dates from the twelfth century – later
rebuilt. The church as a whole was built between 1350 and
1500 in the perpendicular style. The beautiful octagonal spire
is an unusual feature in a Cotswold church. Perhaps the
architect came from Oxford? Another striking feature is the
series of grotesque heads on the outside north wall. Inside, in
the north aisle, there is a niche with a wheel carved in the
stone below it, and the initials S.K., which must once have
held a statue of St Catherine. There is another niche nearby
and one near the pulpit. In the north porch is a highly
unusual niche with depressions for candles and a flue; nearby
is a holy water stoup. The north door of the church dates
from the fourteenth century, and the door to the north porch
is dated 1636. There are three early fifteenth-century bells,
dedicated to St Mary, the mother of Jesus, St Mary Magdalene
and St John the Baptist. In the south porch some fragments of
mediaeval glass have been set in a window.

The church was restored in 1842–43, mainly at the expense
of Lord Sherborne, who provided new open pews. The roof
was rebuilt with a clerestorey added. A gallery on the west

wall, which had an outside entrance, was rebuilt; it was removed in 1948. In 1877 the chancel was rebuilt and a vestry added. The pews were restored in the 1970s.

Over the years the living of Aldsworth was described sometimes as a chapelry, sometimes as a curacy or 'perpetual curacy', and sometimes as a vicarage. It was served at different times by a 'chaplain', a 'curate' or a 'vicar'. At first the church was served from Bibury, but it is not clear where later chaplains, curates or vicars lived: possibly this was in the curate's cottage, sometimes described as two cottages. This is shown on the map of 1799 at the top of Church Lane (where now there is a car park) and described as 'Curate's messuage garden and outbuilding'. For the rest of this section the term 'vicar' will be used, though strictly speaking 'curate' is correct.

From 1736 to 1837 the Dean and Chapter of Christ Church appointed graduates of the college to the living, which was held in plurality with Turkdean, where the vicar lived. However, at least one of the vicars lived in Aldsworth. In 1778 Mr Bowen sent a report to Christ Church: 'the vicarage house is in good repair; I live in it'.

By 1540 the obligation of paying the vicar had been imposed on the lessee of the estate. In 1636 the tenant covenanted to repair the chancel, and this remained the responsibility of the occupier of the Manor until the 1980s. However, a stipend was paid by Christ Church in the seventeenth and eighteenth centuries, and the vicar also had tithes of cows and calves and Easter offerings. At enclosure the vicar was granted 26 acres for his tithes and some rent. The living received an endowment from Queen Anne's Bounty in 1789 and again in 1843. In 1894 the living was worth £150, of which Christ Church paid £107.

In 1835 the Revd Mr Hornsby had to travel 7 miles to Aldsworth and wrote to Christ Church to ask for a house for the vicar. The reply was that the possibility of Aldsworth's being held separately from Turkdean was being considered. Mr Hornsby reported that the two cottages would not be sufficient for the house of a resident minister and reported that the Rectory House was dilapidated.

Early in 1837 the Rectory House was restored completely by Lord Sherborne but was not considered suitable as a residence for the newly appointed vicar, who was assigned a house in Farmington.

For most of the period 1849–88 the Rectory Manor House served as the vicarage. Mr Bellingham lived there in 1851 and Mr Todd in 1871. When Lord Sherborne gave up the tenancy of the estate in 1863, the house was omitted from the new lease and 'granted to the curate'. However, when the house and buildings were offered to the Ecclesiastical Commission in 1872, a grant to establish it as a permanent vicarage could not be obtained. Instead £12 a year was given by the Grants Board towards the cost of housing the vicar. So in 1888 the Rectory House was let together with its land.

In 1848 the Revd John Bellingham had acquired Bridge House near the Manor, presumably for the use of a curate, and in 1871 he sold it to Christ Church. But the Revd A. J. P. Davies, vicar in 1888, found it too small, let it, and rented Taylers Farmhouse. In 1894 Messrs Tayler offered to sell their house, but neither it nor any of the other buildings or sites suggested for a permanent vicarage met with the approval of the diocesan surveyor.

Finally, Lord Sherborne donated a site on high ground a quarter of a mile away north-west of the church and a new vicarage was built in 1905. It is described as being of rock-faced stone with a big tiled roof; the architects were Waller and Sons. So for seventy years Aldsworth had its own vicarage.

In 1976 the living was united with Sherborne-with-Windrush; and Great Barrington with Little Barrington; and the vicar lived in a new vicarage in Windrush.

The first vicar of the united parishes was the Revd Edward Jacson. He was helped by Canon Cratchley, who had retired to Northleach after serving many years as vicar of All Saints, Swindon. He adopted Aldsworth as his own, took most of the services and did a lot of home visiting in the parish. Mr Jacson was succeeded by the Revd Colin McCarter in 1980. The Revd Michael Gee succeeded him in 1991 and the Revd Michael Selwood in 1995.

The vicarage in Aldsworth was sold in 1976.

In 1799 there were four or five cottages on the lane leading to the church. Now there is only one, no. 50, which has been altered and extended.

List of curates appointed

1711	Thomas Biggs
1715	Thomas Aynsworth, AB
1719	Philip Birt, AB
1734	Henry Massey, Clerk
1757	John Saunders, Chaplain
1757	Thomas Bowen
1798	George Illingworth, BD
1807	George Hornsby
1838	Charles William Everett
1839	John George Bellingham
1865	Edward Hallett Todd
1873	Henry Sewell
1881	Edmund Gedge
1888	Albert John Pritchard Davies, BA
1893	George Henry Barrett, BA
1905	Marianus Hay, MA
1926	Griffith Wright Jenkins
	Bennet
	Lawrence
	Pritchard
	Clegg
1976	Edward Jacson
1980	Colin McCarter
1991	Michael Gee
1995	Michael Selwood

The Manor

THE estate in Aldsworth held by the church in Bibury in 1086 consisted of 3 hides of land (approximately 360 acres). The priest and his men had four ploughs. There must therefore have been a house, cottages and farm buildings on the estate at that date. They had probably been there for centuries. In 1151 Bibury Church was 'appropriated' by Oseney Abbey, Oxford. In 1546, not long after the dissolution of the monasteries, the 'impropriate rectory' in Aldsworth, together with the advowson of the church, was handed over to Christ Church, Oxford, a new foundation that was a cathedral and a college combined.

Already before that, in 1544, the Dean (Richard Coxe) and Chapter of the Cathedral granted a lease of the Rectory Manor in Aldsworth to John Blomer of Heythrop for seventy years at a rent of £13 13s 4d. The tenant was to rebuild the ruinous house, provide a bushel of wheat at Easter to make oblations and straw for strewing in the church, and to receive 'honestly' any preacher sent by the Dean and Chapter to preach the word of God in the church. In 1560 a lease of the parsonage, cottage and tithes was granted to Edward Barnard, gentleman, of London for forty years.

In 1612 Henry Powle of Coln St Aldwyns was granted a lease of the manor and parsonage in Aldsworth for the term of three lives.

An early eighteenth-century legal document refers to a 'new-built dwelling house all erected at the only cost and charge of Henry Bote, of stone, timber and other materials, the old being quite ruinated and not habitable, the old tenant not able to repair it. The said new house consisteth of four rooms below stairs and four above with a garret over'. It is difficult to see who this Henry Bote could be, since the name is not recorded anywhere else and the Powle family were tenants from 1612 until 1737. Perhaps 'Henry Bote' was a sub-tenant, or the name possibly could be a mistranscription

The Manor House

of Henry Powle. In a list of inscriptions in the church and the churchyard made in 1785, there are eleven for people with the surname Palmer born between 1685 and 1712. It is likely that this family lived at the Manor. The 1999 edition of *The Buildings of England* describes the Manor in Aldsworth as 'mid-seventeenth century' and thus it is likely to be the house described in the eighteenth-century document – which has no date.

It was probably when Henry Powle (1630–92) was lessee that the Manor House in Aldsworth was built. He was the son of the aforementioned Henry who had bought Williamstrip Manor in Coln St Aldwyns in 1618 and who died in 1642. This younger Henry Powle was MP for Cirencester. He became Speaker of the House of Commons and Master of the Rolls in the reign of William III, and is said to have been that monarch's most trusted adviser. He bought Williamstrip from his elder brother in 1657. After his death in 1692 his daughter Catherine (d. 1714) and her husband Henry Ireton (d. 1711) held a lease of Aldsworth Rectory Manor. They also inherited Williamstrip Manor.

The link between Aldsworth and Williamstrip continued. John Powle and William Forrester who held later leases (see

the list on page 93) were Catherine Ireton's cousins and heirs.
Samuel Blackwell, MP for Cirencester, bought Williamstrip in
about 1760.

It is possible that none of these head lessees actually lived
in Aldsworth. Then, as now, land was bought or leased as an
investment and sub-let.

The leases granted by Christ Church were usually for a
term of seven years. From 1772 the lessee was John Waine
(1738–76), and later his wife Mary. A document of 1723
indicates that a John Waine was a sub-tenant of the Manor in
1712. From 1791 until 1864 Lord Sherborne was the lessee.

Aldsworth Manor was described in 1771 as a three-storey
house of five bays with some twelve rooms.

Lord Sherborne (the 1st Baron) was able to treat the
rectory estate very much as his own. He actually lost the
lease, so that his son later had to apply to Christ Church for
another. He built a stretch of road in front of the house to
complete his green carriageway from Sherborne House to the
turnpike road, so that he could drive directly to the
racecourse at Ladbarrow with his important guest beside
him. A lodge built of ashlar stone with a triangular pediment
was built on the main Cirencester to Burford road. A similar
lodge was built 2 miles to the north on the main Northleach
to Burford road. They were called Allen's Lodges. (Another
lodge half way along the route later became a gamekeeper's
cottage. It was occupied by a Mr Sandles before it was
demolished just after the Second World War.)

The sub-tenants of the Rectory Manor at the time of the
enclosure were William Palphrey and William Hewer.
William Palphrey held Pig Close, the western part of the
rectory estate and Cocklebarrow – 646 acres in all. He was
still there in 1807 with his brother Horatio. Possibly they
lived at Cocklebarrow. William Hewer farmed 245 acres, the
south-east part of Rectory Farm, including the part on the
other side of the main road. In 1821 Adam Craddock farmed
435 acres of the Rectory Farm and Thomas Sadler 148 acres.
In the 1840s and 1850s Richard Waine (1783–1858) farmed 413

acres of Rectory Farm. It is not known where all these tenants lived.

As for the Rectory House itself, the three words most often used to describe it in the Christ Church records are 'large, ancient and ruinous'. In 1835 it was once more in bad repair. The upper floor was said to be unusable: 'one could not tread on it without danger'. In 1837 it was restored completely by Lord Sherborne. From 1849 to 1888 it was usually occupied by the vicar. An attempt was made in 1872 to establish it as a permanent vicarage, but the Ecclesiastical Commission did not consider it suitable.

From about 1890 until 1919, when he retired, the Manor Farm was let to Thomas Reginald Slatter (1868–1930). He married a farmer's daughter Edith Hewer (1872–1949), in 1901 and they had four children, Sara, Lois, Owen and David, born in 1902, 1903, 1906 and 1913.

In 1919 the 621 acres of Manor Farm (sometimes called College Farm) and the Manor House were let to Mr John Burton A'bear (1858–1937), who came with his wife Ada and family from Courtfield Farm, Peppard, Henley-on-Thames. They travelled by train to Fairford and then by horse and wagon. There had been twelve children in the family, two by a first marriage and ten by the second, but the elder son of the first marriage, Jack Bert, had been killed in the 1914–18 war. Thomas Newall, the second eldest, also fought in the war, in the cavalry, but survived, and at the time of the Armistice was in hospital with flu, which he survived also. The eleven A'bear children who came to Aldsworth were Thomas Newall, Winifrid Mary, Edmund Ironsides (known as 'Sides'), Bertha Mary, Albert (who went to Canada and got killed in an accident), George Edgar, Helen (known as Nell), Frederick John, Charles Reginald, Sydney Arthur (known as Ted) and Kathleen Mary.

The family brought their livestock with them – 200 Hampshire Down sheep, six carthorses, a horse and trap, and a horse and van (the horses travelled by road). Some of the family came by car.

Sydney Arthur, known as Ted, was 10 years old when the family came to Aldsworth.

The staff on the farm at that time included the Barnes family – father and son; Jimmy Midwinter, who lived at Chapel Row; John Stevens, who used to clean up round the house and looked after the trap-horse and the trap, and who lived in one of the Manor Farm Cottages; and the shepherd, who lived in the other.

When the eldest sons, Thomas Newall and 'Sides' married, their father put them into farms at Withington and Ablington; but John Burton A'bear died in 1937, leaving four boys and two girls still at home. In 1939 Mr S. J. Phillips asked Charles to manage a farm at Ablington, and then asked Ted to help manage the farms at Kemble. Fred found a job at Daglingworth.

George A'bear (1905–75) was the eldest son left at home when his father died, so he took on the tenancy of Manor Farm in 1937 with his wife Eveline (1903–74). George A'bear farmed Manor Farm for thirty years but had no son to take over the tenancy. In 1970 Christ Church sold the estate with its 620 acres to the Hon. E. R. H. Wills and since then this land has been leased to and farmed by S. J. Phillips and Sons Ltd.

The former Rectory Farmhouse, or Manor, hereafter always called 'The Manor', was sold together with the Manor Lodge and the barns to Captain Peter Percy, TD, in 1975. He and his wife Jean had formerly lived in Bibury. Peter Percy ran a poultry wholesale business from the big barn behind the house. Refrigerated lorries laden with chickens and turkeys would come and go at all times of the day and night.

The house was stripped of the ivy that covered it and extensively restored. The porch was altered with a flight of steps up to it and the house was floodlit so that its appearance was completely changed. Inside the house was redecorated with considerable style and flair. The Percys were outgoing and hospitable. They had two beautiful daughters, Vanessa and Joanna, who were fashion models. Joanna was 'deb. of the year' in the early 1980s. Peter took his responsibility for the church chancel seriously and supported the church in many ways. He also founded the Aldsworth branch of the British Legion. Unfortunately the poultry business failed and the Percys had to leave in 1986.

The Manor House was sold to Mr and Mrs M. Hulbert. The big barn was sold separately and converted to two houses, Manor Barn and Aldstead. The lodge was also sold separately. The pair of semi-detached farm cottages on the Cirencester road were built just before 1919.

Leases of Aldsworth Rectory Manor granted by
Christ Church

1544	John Blomer of Heythrop
1560	Edward Barnard of London
1612	Henry Powle of Coln St Aldwyns
1636	Henry Powle
1680	Henry Powle
1695	Henry Ireton and his wife Catherine, the only daughter and heir of Henry Powle
1717	John Powle
1723	John Powle
1724	John Powle
1730	John Powle
1737	John Powle
1744	William Forrester
1751	John Needham and Robert Henley
1766	Samuel Blackwell
1772	John Waine
1779	Mary Waine, widow of John
1786	Mary Waine
1809	James Dutton, 1st Baron Sherborne
1823	John Dutton, 2nd Baron Sherborne
1834	John Dutton
1836	John Dutton
1843	John Dutton

1850	John Dutton
1857	John Dutton
1864	Charles John Howard, 27th Earl of Suffolk and Berkshire
1970	Sold to the Hon. E. R. H. Wills – 620 acres for £180,000

Wall Farm

WALL Farm as such is not referred to in the text of *Domesday Book* (1087) itself, but the 2 hides held in 1086 by the King's thane Alfward have been identified as being 'at Wall', a site to the north end of Aldsworth village. The full entry in *Domesday Book* runs: 'Alfward son of Reinbald holds Aldsworth, Balki held it. 2 hides which pay tax. In Lordship 1 plough, 4 villagers and 2 small holders with 2 ploughs, 1 slave. The value was 40s now 30s.' Balki was described as 'The Dane' in a charter of 1133.

It is probable that Wall Farm was inhabited in Romano-British times, and possible that it had been occupied long before that. Cirencester was the largest town in Roman Britain after London, and the area round it shows remains of many Roman villas, farms and roads. It is known that after the Roman legions were withdrawn from Britain in AD 410,

Wall Farm

towns were abandoned. The population fell. It was an unstable time with no firm government to keep order and prevent looters and raiders from helping themselves. There was a tendency for people to live in fortified farmsteads on high ground where they could defend themselves and their animals and possessions, as they had done in earlier centuries. It is possible that Wall Farm was one such settlement. It is on high ground with a reliable water supply. The name 'Aldsworth' gives a clue. It is possible that 'Aldsworth' is a corruption of 'Aldworth' or 'Ealdworth', meaning old enclosure. The unusual name 'Wall' gives another clue. It is possible that there was a wall around the settlement when the Anglo-Saxons first arrived.

In 1133 King Henry I granted the estate, with other property formerly held by Alfward's father, to Cirencester Abbey, which was granted free warren in 1252. The abbey held the estate until the dissolution of the monasteries by King Henry VIII in 1536–39. In 1543 it was granted to Richard Andrews and Nicholas Temple, and in 1547 Richard sold it to William Blomer of Cowley. After William's death in 1554 the estate with the tithes of wool and lambs passed to his brother-in-law, William Colley of Buscot (Berks), who died in 1557, leaving as his heir his son Giles, a minor. Giles Colley (d. 1558) was succeeded by his brother Thomas. After Thomas' death in 1603 the estate passed to his son Thomas (d. 1616), whose son Thomas sold it to John Blomer of Hatherop in 1637. John died in 1638 and the estate passed to his son William, who released it in 1669 to his elder brother John. It then passed with Hatherop Manor and in 1764 was owned by Sir John Webb. Wall Farm, which was apparently sold by 1785, was part of Lord Sherborne's estate in 1793 when he was allotted 240 acres for the farm and 65 acres for the tithes.

Richard Collett, a tenant of 504 acres, farmed the land around Wall Farmhouse at the time of the enclosure.

In 1799 William Garne, aged 56, came to Aldsworth from Sherborne to farm the newly enclosed land of Wall Farm.

When he died two years later in 1801 he left a widow and nine children. His eldest son William (1781–1857) was left to run Wall Farm with the help of his two brothers. In 1839 Wall Farm comprised 477 acres. By then William II also farmed Blackpits. He married Marianne Waine in 1809. His brother Thomas married Mary Gillett from Woeful Lake. She died young and the five children of the marriage were brought up at Wall Farm by their grandmother and their aunt.

William and Marianne Garne also had nine children. The youngest son Robert (1825–1900) took over from his father when the latter died in 1857. He lived at Blackpits, and farmed Blackpits and Wall Farm together. Shortly after his death, his heir W. T. Garne gave up the tenancy of both farms.

In 1861 Wall Farmhouse was occupied by John George, his wife Sarah and their four children: presumably he was farm manager. Later the farm manager living there was Mr Blake. It is said that Robert Garne at Blackpits would open his bedroom window in the morning and shout instructions to Mr Blake a quarter of a mile away.

From early in the twentieth century until 1940 the tenancy of Wall Farm was held by the Jefferies family, who were related to the Jefferies family who ran a nursery garden in Cirencester. They gave the Wilcoxes two pear trees that are still growing on the wall of the farmhouse.

Mr and Mrs Alfred Wilcox came to Wall Farm from Ampney St Mary in 1940 with their 7-month-old son John. With them came Alfred Vincent, who worked for them, and his family, including his teenage sons Cecil, Wally and Leonard. They walked the cows to Wall Farm in the morning and milked them there in the afternoon. Leonard later became the Wilcoxes' right-hand man on the farm.

Another son, David, was born to the Wilcoxes in 1942. He was educated at King's School, which occupied Sherborne House from 1947 to 1966. David married Beryl Rhymes from Cirencester in 1965.

In 1968, when his parents retired to Bampton, David became the tenant of Wall Farm. His brother John farmed the family's farm at Wootton near Abingdon, until his early death in 1992. David and Beryl have a son, Anthony, and a daughter Sarah. Sarah married Tom Matthews, a farmer from Uffington, Oxfordshire, in 1996.

In 1982 the Wilcoxes were able to buy their farm from the heirs of Lord Sherborne. They maintain a herd of pedigree Friesian dairy cows. They also rear pigs. David, like his father before him, is a churchwarden.

The left-hand side of the farmhouse is very old and partly made of wattle and daub with an ancient cellar. The right-hand side of the house is an early nineteenth-century addition. The barn on the right dates from 1845. The 1799 enclosure map shows buildings arranged in a relatively tight square around a yard, and the farm still has that structure at its core today. Until the late 1960s the yard was cobbled.

Besides the pair of cottages called Pear Tree Cottages on the green, there is another pair near the house, and a single cottage on the west side of the lane. A strip of land here was named Maul Croft in 1799. No buildings are shown on it on the map of that date, but evidence of buildings has been found, which must be the cottages said to have been demolished here to make way for the new carriageway from Sherborne Park in the 1790s.

Blackpits Farm

O N the 1799 enclosure map an unnamed house and farmyard are shown on the site of Blackpits House. The tenant at the time of the enclosure was Lawrence Smith (1746–1816), who farmed 570 acres to the north and east. Part of this land gave its name to the house and farm (see Appendix B).

The present Blackpits House is said to have been built for Robert Garne in 1854, by his father William, using stone from demolished buildings nearby.

Robert Garne, born in 1825, was the grandson of William Garne who came to Aldsworth from Sherborne in 1799. He was a very successful farmer and businessman who enjoyed the years of prosperity for tenant farmers in the middle of the nineteenth century, but also managed to increase his land holding and prosper in the years of depression between 1878 and 1900. In the fine house built by his father he enjoyed a standard of living equal to that of the gentry and at the end of his life he was described as a 'Yeoman Prince'. He was a batchelor who lived with his sisters Elizabeth and Jane. When they died in 1885 and 1886, his nephew W. T. Garne and wife Susanna lived in the house with him. They had three children and had previously lived in a house nearby. Susanna died in 1892 and four years later W.T. married the housekeeper, Miss Miller.

W. T. Garne, already wealthy, inherited his uncle's fortune when the latter died in 1900. He gave up the tenancies of Blackpits and Wall Farm and bought and moved into what is now known as Taylers Farmhouse.

From 1900 the tenant of Blackpits was Mr Tom Rich, a Cornish Nonconformist. It was he who built the Methodist Chapel in Aldsworth in 1907.

When Mr Rich retired in the late 1920s, no tenant could be found to farm the land at Blackpits. This was a time of agricultural depression when it was difficult for farmers to make a profit. The house was let to the agent of the Sherborne Estate. When Mr S. J. Phillips (John Phillips) took it over in 1930 he had the land rent-free for a year, and for 2s 6d to 7s 6d an acre after that.

Mr and Mrs Phillips lived at Kemble, not at Blackpits House, which continued to be let. Their elder son Gregory took over Blackpits in 1938, but left at the beginning of the war to serve his country in the armed forces. During the war the house was occupied by a Major Edwards and family. The land was farmed together with Woeful Lake and Kilkenny.

When Gregory Phillips returned from the war he married Helen Wakefield, whose family farmed near Burford. They moved into Blackpits House, where they lived for more than fifty years. They had three children, Carol, John and Lavinia. After the death of the 7th Lord Sherborne in 1982 they were able to buy the freehold of Blackpits.

The fine range of stone buildings behind Blackpits House dates from the mid-nineteenth century. The large drier barn was built in 1958 and the other in 1983.

There is a pair of farm cottages behind the house: one is occupied by Keith Hull who, like his parents before him, worked on the farm, and the other by Mr Peter Stratton, head groom to Mr Phillips for many years. His wife Mollie died in November 2000. There is another pair of cottages by the Sherborne road. One is occupied by the shepherd Mr Alex John Inglis and his family. The other was occupied by Harry Smith, who worked on the farm for twenty-five years before retiring to Cirencester.

Taylers Farmhouse

JOHN Waine built what is now known as Taylers Farmhouse by altering an earlier building, described in 1799 as 'House Bakehouse, Gardens etc', belonging to Thomas Waine, his uncle. A Georgian-style three-storey block with a slate roof in the form of a pyramid was added to the existing building, probably as a separate house. The date this house was built, 1831, is shown on the weathervane, and the initials J.W. were also, until recently, attached to it.

This John Waine was born in 1789, the son of Richard Waine (1765–1821) who lived at the site of the present pub, the Sherborne Arms. In the population census of 1841 John was described as a stable keeper. He never married, and in 1851 he was described as a landed proprietor with one servant/housekeeper, and in a later trade directory as a gentleman.

It seems likely that John Waine bought the whole site from his cousins and invested in the brewery, which replaced the bakery at about that time. A malthouse was built behind the house and an enormous cellar built under the garden. In the 1841 and 1851 censuses a William Waine is recorded as being a brewer. In 1851 William was described as being 45, a farmer of 48 acres, with two servants, one brewer, one maltster and one carter, with a wife Mary and three daughters, Rebecca, Mary and Jane. This William, born in 1806, was the eldest son of Richard Waine (b. 1783) and a grandson of Thomas Waine, and it is likely that he and his family lived at Taylers Farmhouse. The eldest daughter, Rebecca, died aged 20 in 1854 and is buried in the churchyard.

John died in 1858, probably leaving his property to his brother Joseph. The house and brewery were sold to John Walker Tayler from Northleach. William and Mary left the village, but it is not known where they went.

John Walker Tayler (1830–79) and his wife Elizabeth Mary (1829–1908) had nine children, Thomas, John, Marion, Elizabeth, Edward, Helen, Ernest, Frank and Fred. Their son 'Frederick George' who 'fell asleep' in 1888 aged 20 is buried with them in the churchyard in Aldsworth. They altered the house – probably joining two houses into one. Unlikely as it seems, old photographs show that they moved the front door one bay to the left. John was described as a wine and spirit merchant as well as a brewer, a maltster and a farmer of 64 acres. When he died in 1879 his widow remained. A trade directory of 1888 records a Mrs Tayler, brewer, in Aldsworth. She died in 1908, but by then the brewery business had moved to Northleach. Taylers Farmhouse was let for a while to the vicar, the Revd A. J. Davies. He is said to have died in the front bedroom, although the census of 1891 gives his age in that year as 31. In 1900 or soon after, the house was sold to Mr W. T. Garne of Blackpits House, who moved in with his second wife.

W. T. Garne had inherited his uncle's fortune and wished to live like a gentleman. A new wing was added to the house, giving a drawing room and extra bedroom. A conservatory was added, bay windows were put in, a new staircase was built and a tennis court was made. Stables and a coach house were also added. W. T. Garne bought Green Farm and rented Swyre Farm. He bred shorthorn cattle and sheep.

After W. T.'s death in 1925 his son Will moved into the house with his wife, son and six daughters. They lived there (with W. T. Garne's widow until she died) until Will Garne's death in 1967.

Will Garne was interested in hunting, and in breeding and showing cattle and sheep, and black and red game cocks. He kept the very last flock of Cotswold sheep.

On the death of Will Garne, his estate was split up and sold. Taylers Farmhouse, by then in need of renovation, was sold to Major and Mrs Ruck-Keene. Major Ruck-Keene was an officer in the Ox and Bucks Light Infantry, and was a friend of Charles Dutton, 7th Lord Sherborne, with whom he used to go shooting.

After a few years the Ruck-Keenes made a new house for themselves by altering and adding to the stables, using part of the malting house as a garage. Taylers Farmhouse was sold in about 1973 to Mr and Mrs Biden. In 1978 the Bidens sold Taylers Farmhouse to the present occupants.

Stable End, the house built by the Ruck-Keenes, had several owners after they had left to live in Cornwall in the mid-1980s.

The Cock House, between Taylers Farmhouse and Smiths Corner, where Will Garne had carefully groomed and prepared his black and red game cocks for the show ring, was sold separately and is now a holiday cottage.

Smiths Corner

THE building at Smiths Corner, which is shown, though not named, on the enclosure map of 1799, was home to a family who were yeomen farmers in Aldsworth in the eighteenth century and perhaps before. At the time of the enclosure Lawrence Smith (1746–1816) was a tenant of Lord

Sherborne, farming 570 acres. It seems from inscriptions on gravestones in the churchyard that he died in 1816 aged 70, leaving a wife, Sarah, aged 58, daughters Sarah and Joan, aged 20 and 17, and a son, Lawrence, aged 17.

Also shown on the 1799 map is an area of just over an acre named Smiths Paddock, where nos. 1–6 The Approach were built in the late 1940s. The barn and area beside Smiths Corner was known as Smiths Yard until 1967.

William Garne took over the farm when Lawrence Smith died and it was renamed Blackpits. However, the survival of the name Smiths Yard suggests that the widow and children stayed on in their home as small-holders or employees. Sarah, widow of Lawrence, died in 1840 aged 82, and their son Lawrence in 1878 aged 79. Their daughters Sarah and Joan died unmarried in Northleach in 1874 and 1869, aged 78 and 70.

Smiths Farmhouse and Smiths Yard were bought from Lord Sherborne by W. T. Garne in 1900 or soon after. The farmhouse became the herdsman's cottage and the other buildings were adapted for W. T. Garne's herd of prize winning pedigree shorthorn cattle. When W. T. Garne died in 1925 his son William succeeded him. When he died in 1967 his property and land was split up and sold.

Smiths Corner was bought by a Dan Air pilot, Mr Bond, and his wife before being sold to Mr and Mrs C. Travis in the 1970s. They sold it to the present occupants in 1997.

The garden across the road from Smiths Corner was bought from the Sherborne Estate in the early 1990s by Mr and Mrs Travis. It had previously been a garden used by Dennis Harris of Chapel Row.

When the estate of Will Garne was split up and sold in 1967 the house adjoining Smiths Corner with its very old barn and garden was renamed 'Waylands Barn' (after Wayland the Smith of legend) by its new owners, Miss Margaret Graham and Miss Dagma Andersen. They had been Principal and Head of English in a Teacher Training College in Bristol. Margaret Graham died a few years later. Miss

Andersen lived on at Waylands Barn until her death in 1997. She was a scholar of English Literature and a supporter of the church. She ran the Ladies Circle, which met once a month in the barn.

Part of Smiths Yard adjoining Waylands Barn was sold separately and a house called Well House was built on it in the early 1970s. It was bought soon after by Miss Frances Punchard. She kept bull mastiffs, which she used to show, in the yard behind. When she died the house was unoccupied for several years and became very dilapidated. It was bought and rebuilt in 1998–9.

The Post Office

THE present Post Office was built in 1967 on land which long ago had been occupied by the family of Mrs R. Crewe, the present postmistress. It was bought by them in the 1950s from Lord Sherborne. The present Post Office replaced one near the main Cirencester to Burford road.

The Post Office stands on the site where the village blacksmith once had his home and forge. On the 1799 map this plot is marked 'Henry Collett (Blacksmith) Homestead'. On it an L-shaped building immediately opposite Smiths Corner and a further small building are shown. Presumably the forge was here as well as the house. Also shown on the map is a half-acre piece of land called Collett's Close on the right-hand side of the lane leading to the school.

The parish records and the gravestones in the churchyard show that there were many people of the surname Collett living in the village during the last two centuries. Many blacksmiths of that name are recorded, and there were blacksmiths of that name in other villages nearby also. The last blacksmith in Aldsworth was Cecil Collet at no. 22.

It is not known when the house and forge on the site of the present Post Office were demolished, but in the first half

of the twentieth century the site was a vegetable garden (for Taylers Farmhouse).

Mrs Crewe moved to the site of the present Post Office in 1967 with her father Robert Collett, husband Reginald and son Nigel. Robert died in 1976, and Reginald, who worked for Smiths Industries in Cheltenham, died in 1992. Nigel married Shirley Lock from Cirencester in 1988.

Hill House and Hill Crest, opposite the Post Office, were built in the 1960s. Hill Crest was owned by Mrs Joan Ash and her two sons. Later it was bought by Mr and Mrs G. Weaver. He is a retired bank manager. They moved from Fairfield, another house in the village. Hill House was bought by Mr and Mrs L. Terry.

Whitegates was a cottage or pair of cottages in the eighteenth century.

Green Farm

Green Farm House faces south over a small triangular green where there was a well and where a war memorial was erected after the 1914–18 war. The house in earlier times faced west on to the lane – the arch of the main doorway can be seen in the wall. The lower half of the wall gives the impression that there was once a timber-framed house here. It

Green Farm

probably dated from Tudor times or earlier but has clearly
been added to and altered many many times. In 1766 it was
described as a substantial well-built stone messuage with a
malt-house. Behind the house was a dovecote.

The earliest mention of Green Farm (though not by name)
is in 1638, when Thomas Lawrence, described as a yeoman in
1608, and Anthony Fettiplace granted an estate of $5\frac{1}{2}$
yardlands (approximately 165 acres) to Thomas and Matthew
Bennett of Wiltshire. From 1676 the estate was held by
various members of the Greenwood family. In 1766 Charles
Greenwood sold the estate to John Waine (1738–76), whose
family had had a lease of it since 1717 at least.

John Waine and his wife Mary Evans had two sons,
Thomas and Richard, and a daughter, Mary. When John died
in 1776 at the early age of 37 his children were aged 13, 11
and 9. He left Green Farm to his eldest son Thomas
(1764–1815). The enclosure map of 1799 shows that the 200
acres of land stretched along the side of the road to Burford.
A building is shown on the site of the present pub,
surrounded by enclosed plots of land of unusual shape: there
was also an area of land on the Ladbarrow side of the road.
In 1799 Thomas Waine also owned several plots of land in the
village, the sites of Green Garden, Howard's Cottage and the
Old Bakery. Thomas Waine also owned the site of what is
now Taylers Farmhouse, which was then described as
'House, Bakehouse, Gardens etc'.

Thomas Waine and his wife Mary Carter had nine
children. Two sons and a daughter died as infants. Two
daughters married. Of the remaining four sons, John
(1782–1849) succeeded his father at Green Farm; Richard was
a baker, and later farmed the Rectory Manor Farm; Thomas
was a maltster who left Aldsworth in about 1830 and settled
in Burford; and William (1795–) also left the village.

John Waine (1782–1849), who succeeded his father Thomas
at Green Farm in 1815, married Susanna Fletcher of Sherborne
in 1806. Susanna died in 1826 at the age of 40, giving birth to
their fourteenth child, according to the inscription on her

gravestone in the churchyard. It seems John married again, as another gravestone is inscribed 'Phoebe, second wife of John Waine, died 1836'. The eleven surviving children of John and Susanna were Thomas, Giles, Mary, Joseph, John, James, Susanna, Elizabeth, Anne, Charles and George.

By 1851 the eldest son, Thomas, was living in Bourton-on-the-Water, married with three children and described as a landed proprietor; in that same year the fourth son, John, was married with one child and farming 105 acres in Great Rissington. Joseph had married in 1840 and set up a shop in Aldsworth, which by 1851 had become the village bakery. Mary and Ann had both married in 1845. Giles, the second son of John and Susanna, succeeded his father at Green Farm in 1849. In 1851 he was living at home with two of his sisters and three of his brothers. Giles, born in 1809, married Martha Craddock (1818–1907), and had a daughter Lucy, born in 1855, and a son John Charles, born in 1861. Elizabeth, Susanna, James, Charles and George moved out of the village but all were buried in Aldsworth, apparently unmarried, between 1865 and 1880.

When Giles died in 1866 his son was still a child. The Houlton family of Ladbarrow took over the running of Green Farm. John Houlton, the second son of the family, born in 1848, married Giles' daughter Lucy in 1874 and moved into Green Farm House. By 1881 John and Lucy had three children – but, according to an inscription on a gravestone in the churchyard, 'Lucy, dearly loved wife of John Houlton, fell asleep in Jesus, June 23rd 1882 aged 27 years' together with her infant daughter, Lucy Fanny, aged 30 hours. John Houlton returned to live at Ladbarrow.

Fate had not been kind to John Charles: his father had died when he was 5 and his only sister when he was 21. By then his mother, who had been 43 when he was born, was in her sixties, and all his many Waine uncles and aunts were dead. The 1880s and 1890s were difficult years for farmers. In 1897 the land of Green Farm was sold and John Charles moved away to Farmington.

A few years later Mr W. T. Garne (who lived at what is now Taylers Farmhouse) bought the land and also the house. The whole estate was very run down. After the death in 1907 of Martha Waine (who still lived in the house), Mr Garne's shepherd, Jim Wilcox, lived at Green Farm. His sister and family, the Baxters, also lived there. One of the schoolteachers, Miss Price, lodged there in the 1930s. The shepherd Jack Bond also lived there.

Green Farm House and the field in front were bought in 1963 by Mr and Mrs F. Houlton. Frank Houlton's father William, son of Thomas Houlton, was born at Ladbarrow in 1859. One of William's earliest memories was of hunting for golden sovereigns under the grandstand on the racecourse after it had been demolished. William married Jane Lane, daughter of William Lane of Broadfield Farm, a famous breeder and exporter of Cotswold sheep who was a great rival of the Garne family, his cousins. The 700 acres of Broadfield Farm lay just to the west of Aldsworth Parish.

Frank's parents, William and Jane, took over Broadfield Farm and there Frank was born and spent his childhood. During the First World War, when all the men had left to fight, it was rather a shock for Frank, at the age of 12, to be taken away from boarding school and set to plough the fields with only the aid of a pensioner who helped him turn the plough. It was an even greater shock to return to school two years later.

Frank married May, who came from a Herefordshire farming family. They farmed for many years at Bibury and had one daughter, Molly. It was a particular pleasure for them to retire to Green Farm House as Frank was related by marriage to the Waine family. May maintained a lovely garden there and created beautiful flower arrangements for the church. She died in 1997, aged 93, having survived her husband by several years. Molly then sold Green Farm House to the present occupants.

In 1969 Molly had purchased some of the Green Farm outbuildings, including the dovecote and the small barn, and in 1976 converted the dovecote into a cottage for herself called 'Tallet Cottage'.

The fine large barn (now Brockton Barn) next to Green Farmhouse dates from the mid-nineteenth century. When Will Garne died in 1967 his estate was split up. Mr Michael Henriques of Winson bought the land of Green Farm, and the barn, in which he installed a grain drier. A few years later Mr and Mrs C. Cliff bought the barn and land. After the barn had been converted to a house they moved in with their two small daughters and named the property Harvest Farm. They ran various business enterprises from here, from herb growing and breeding Limousin cattle to letting their land, complete with jumps, for riding events.

The Keive was built opposite Harvest Barn for Mrs Cliff's parents, Mr and Mrs Martin Sharp. In the 1980s another house was built behind it. The Cliffs moved to the Keive and the Sharps to the new house and Harvest Barn was sold to Mr and Mrs K. Dyke, who renamed it Brocton Barn. The Dykes later sold it to Dr and Mrs D. Turtle.

The Cliffs moved to the Fairford area in the early 1990s after the death of Mr and Mrs Sharp, and the houses and land were sold to Mr and Mrs G. Copley.

The Copleys sold the Keive in 1996 and moved into the house behind it.

There has been a cottage on the site of Gassons View since some time in the nineteenth century. It was sold separately after the break-up of the Green Farm estate. Mrs Bevin, widow of the headteacher Mr Bevin, lived there in the 1950s. In the 1970s and 1980s it was occupied by Mr and Mrs Tom Mace.

The Green Garden is on the west side of the Green by the war memorial, on the site of what was once the garden and rick-yard of Green Farm.

The Garne family kept this site, which had been their orchard and fruit garden, and a bungalow was then built there for Will Garne's widow Frances and daughter Susanna (Sue, b. 1910). After Mrs Garne's death in 1973 another of her daughters, Phyllis (Mrs P. Pike, b. 1912), came to live with her sister Sue, where they still reside in 2000. Sue loves gardening and for many years supplemented their income by the sale of her produce at the Women's Institute Friday market at Cirencester. She had her first garden in the family home at Ablington at the age of 5 and for her ninetieth birthday requested a wheelbarrow.

Green Garden Cottage did not belong to Green Farm. It is shown on the 1799 map and labelled 'Joseph Mosson, messuage and garden (purchased of Lord Sherborne)'. Later it was two cottages and at one time three. One was occupied in 1980, by Mr and Mrs Henly. It was modernised after their death, then changed hands several times. Since 1992 Mr and Mrs Gardner have owned and occupied it. The garden used to extend further west until a portion was bought by the occupants of Wheelwrights in the 1990s. Here there is a shallow circular depression, which was once used as a cockpit, according to a former inhabitant of the house.

The Old School House

THE School House stands on the site of the former inn, the Sherborne Arms which was 'suppressed' in 1845 (see Appendix C). It is probable that the inn was very old and that it was totally demolished. In 1799 the tenant was Thomas Allchin, and in 1841 Humphrey Porter, aged 40, who had a wife Mary and ten children.

The School House was built by Lord Sherborne at the same time as Aldsworth Church of England School – that is, in 1853. The Christ Church records state that the schoolmistress received £45 and a house rent-free maintained by Lord Sherborne. The house was occupied by the teacher or the headteacher when there was more than one, until the school closed in 1979. The last teacher was James Harber, who died in 1979 soon after the school was closed. Since then the house has changed hands several times.

Brightwells Cottage was built by Lord Sherborne in the late nineteenth century as a reading-room. In the 1930s it served as a sort of youth club. In the 1940s it was the headquarters of the Home Guard.

By the 1950s the reading-room was derelict and unused. It was sold in the early 1960s.

Home Close acquired that name in the 1980s. The site is marked 'Home Close' on the map of 1799 and two buildings are shown on it. The area behind it is labelled 'Piece behind the Jockey Stable', so these buildings must have been stables. The first was converted to a row of three cottages. In the 1930s Harry Bishop lived in the first cottage. Ken Stevens and Ewart Cook both lived in one of them for a while. For many years Thomas Haines (1868–1951) and his wife Maria (1873–1941) lived in the end cottage, and from 1920 they ran the Post Office from there. It was also a shop. Their daughters Maud and Elsie continued to run the Post Office in the 1950s, until it was taken over by Mrs Crewe in 1959. In the 1980s, when the cottages were being converted to one house, bits of straw and bran were found in the walls.

The second building on Home Close is called Wheelwrights. From the 1920s to the 1950s it was occupied by Mr Rufus Harris and his wife. He was a smallholder and also a carpenter and undertaker. In the shed behind the house he repaired wheels together with the blacksmith Cecil Collett. Fred Saunders and Tom Edgington helped him. Rufus Harris kept pigs, hens and two cows on a smallholding on the side of the Ladbarrow road and did a milk round. The milking shed was behind the house. Mrs Crewe remembers helping to make the butter as a child.

It was in this house that Mr John Bond (Jack) lodged towards the end of his life. He died in 1981 aged 85 and was buried with a bit of wool in his coffin 'so that the Good Lord would know he was a shepherd'. A photograph of him holding two Cotswold lambs can be seen in the Sherborne Arms. In his younger days Jack Bond's hobby was fairground merry-go-rounds. He had one of his own which he would

take to fêtes and fairs and he also had his own traction engine
– his pride and joy. The house was sold in the 1980s.

The tenant of Little Mullions in 1799 was Joseph Meers. In
the early twentieth century it was occupied by Mr Robert
Collett (1886–1976) and his wife Florence (1888–1946). Robert,
a plumber, worked for Godwin Pumps of Quenington and
was instrumental in bringing the first piped water supply to
Aldsworth from Windrush in 1920. His detailed knowledge
of where exactly all the pipes had been laid across the fields
later proved invaluable to the farmers. In 1959 Robert's
daughter, Mrs Rose Crewe, took over the Post Office, which
was transferred to their house from the Haines home nearby.
A new Post Office was built in 1967 on another site and Mrs
Crewe moved there with her father, husband and son.

From Little Mullions a footpath leads uphill to the Old
Bakery. The house on the left, no. 22, used to be a forge run
by Cecil Collett, the last blacksmith in Aldsworth. Cecil
Collett moved to Quenington in 1960 and died in 1970. In the
1980s, when it was occupied by Mrs Pinchin, whose husband,
Reg, used to be the postman, no. 22 was a picturesque old
cottage in an orchard, and the site of the forge could be seen.

The Old Bakery

THE site of the Old Bakery belonged in 1799 to Thomas
Waine of Green Farm. The enclosure map showed no
building on it then. The present house was probably built by
or for Joseph Waine and his wife Jane Collett, who married in
1839. Joseph, born in 1812, was the third son of John and
Susanna Waine of Green Farm and Jane was probably one of
the family of Henry Collett the blacksmith.

Joseph and Jane had seven children, Elizabeth, Susanna,
Ellen Jane, Mary Ann, William, James and John. In 1841
Joseph was described as a grocer, but in 1851 as a shopkeeper
and baker. The bakery probably replaced the Waine family

bakehouse, which became a brewery at about this time. When Joseph died in 1854 at the age of 42, his widow and children continued to run the bakery with the help of a 'journeyman baker'. By 1871 Jane was described as a draper as well as a baker. Elizabeth and Mary Ann were her assistants, and William and John were the bakers. By then Susanna and Ellen had married and James had also left home. Mary Ann and William both died aged 26 in 1872 and 1874. Their mother Jane died in 1889 aged 77. In 1891 the grocery and bakery was run by John, the youngest of the family, born in 1853. His sister Elizabeth was keeping house and there were also two nephews, Ernest, aged 22, a grocer's assistant, and Harry aged 16, an apprentice. Another baker lodged in the house with them.

John is probably the John Waine buried in the churchyard who died in 1914. It is not known what happened to Ernest and Harry but by the early 1920s the bakery had been sold.

The bakery was taken over by Mr Charles Legg. He delivered bread from a horse-drawn van, not only in Aldsworth, but also in other villages, including Coln St Aldwyns. The bakery closed in the 1950s. After Mr Legg's death his daughter Marjorie continued to live in the house with her husband Ted Fowler, who was head bus-driver for C. J. Howse and later for Marchants Coaches. In the 1960s Mr and Mrs Fowler opened a small shop. When her husband died in 1978 Mrs Fowler moved to Cheltenham.

The house and bakery building adjoining were sold to Major and the Hon. Mrs Cowie (Nigel and Juliana), who moved in with their two small children. Major Cowie was tragically killed in a car crash in 1991. In 1994 the Hon. Mrs Cowie married Christopher Grose.

On the opposite side of the road from the Old Bakery, next to the school, is a house called Park Place. In the 1920s to the 1950s it was a shop run by Mrs Salvage. An inscription on a gravestone in the churchyard records: 'Ethelbert L. Salvage died April 2nd 1955 aged 73 years, rest in peace' and 'Florence Lucy Salvage died 21st December 1974 aged 90 years. Reunited'. The shop was a general store selling groceries, sweets and other goods. You could also have a bath for a penny before the war when few houses had bathrooms.

Mr Salvage had in mid-life suffered in a road accident on the Burford road. A penny in his pocket was driven into his leg, which became gangrenous and had to be amputated. He became a cobbler and would sit in a little shed, with a bucket of water beside him to soften the leather, and mend shoes. He was popular with the boys playing tops on the playground as he could put a new tip on a top if necessary.

Mrs Salvage gave up the shop some years before her death: it was then run by a Mrs Porter. In the 1980s Park Place was sold.

Windrush House, The Paddock, Howard's Cottage

UNTIL the early 1980s Windrush House was a large barn. It was called Howard's Barn because the tenant was Joseph Howard (1863–1951), a smallholder who lived in a cottage on the other side of the road. He kept pigs, cows and poultry, and had some grazing land behind 'The Barracks' as well as a paddock beside the barn itself. The Phillips family of Blackpits took over his property after his death.

The site of this barn was one of several plots of land in the middle of the village held in 1799 by John Tayler, a tenant of Lord Sherborne who had 88 acres in all. He may be the John Tayler who had a house, garden and stable directly between Blackpits and Taylers Farmhouse, demolished in the mid-nineteenth century.

In the early 1980s Gregory Phillips sold Howard's Barn and the paddock next to it to Mr and Mrs M. Biden. A few years later the paddock was resold and a house built on it.

By this time the Bidens had converted Howard's Barn to a house. After a few years it was sold and renamed Windrush

Barn. It was sold again in 1995 and is now called Windrush House.

'The Paddock' was built around 1984. It had one occupier before being sold to the present owners, Mr and Mrs P. Stewart, who retired to Aldsworth after living in Brazil and Spain.

Howard's Cottage opposite The Paddock was built in 1847 by John Waine. There may have been a house there before. It has been altered and extended since. One of the Tayler family, John Osborne Tayler, lived there in 1885 when the house was described as 'Aldsworth Villa'. For the first half of the twentieth century Joey Howard lived there as described above. He died in 1951 aged 88. His wife had died in 1934. The house was bought by Gregory Phillips and renovated. During its renovation lots of top-quality wiring was found in the roof, connected to numerous bell pushes of the kind used to summon servants, although the house was small.

From 1956 to 1962 Mr and Mrs Taylor (Kennedy and Muriel) lived at Howard's Cottage. Two of their sons, Ian and Duncan, were born while they were there. In 1962 they exchanged houses with Mr and Mrs Garne, who were retiring from farming at Cocklebarrow. From 1967 Mrs Arthur Garne's sister Frances, widow of Will Garne, and her nieces, Sue and Phyllis, lived next door at Green Garden. Arthur Garne died in 1981 aged 91 and his wife Helen in 1983 aged 93. For a while the house was let.

Howard's Cottage was bought by Mr and Mrs Taylor towards the end of his farming career. In 1990 they retired there, thus returning to their former home after 28 years at Cocklebarrow.

On the corner between Windrush House and Green Farm are two cottages, Ivy Cottage and Chestnut Corner.

From 1895 a Mr Porter lived in Ivy Cottage. His job was carting stone for building, and also mending the roads. Behind the house was a stable for eight shire horses. Opposite it was a pigsty, toilets and a cart-shed, also a plough to push back the verges. Only the main roads were tarmaced in the 1930s; the rest were surfaced with stones.

The Chapel

THE Wesleyan Methodist Chapel was built in 1907 by
Mr Tom Rich from Cornwall, who lived at Blackpits Farm
at that time. It is a well-designed stone building with a small
spire. It had an attractive interior. Mr Rich must have been
known to the Lawry family of Macaroni Downs Farm, who
were also Methodists from Cornwall. Some of them,
including John Phillips, the grandson, probably attended
Aldsworth Chapel from the start. John Phillips and his wife
Ruth would have attended the Chapel regularly when they
lived at Cocklebarrow from 1914 to 1918.

Over the years the congregation dwindled, and by the
1980s the Chapel was no longer used for services. It was
converted in the 1980s, and the present owners let rooms for
bed and breakfast.

Chapel Row, a row of four cottages, dates from much
earlier times than the Chapel. No. 28, slightly larger than

The Old Chapel

nos. 29 and 30, was the first to be modernised and the owner acquired the strip of garden behind the four cottages to add to the piece in front.

The Mander family used to live at no. 29 and no. 31. William Mander (1879–1947) was sexton at the church and rang the bells. Mrs Mander at no. 31 was a washerwoman in the early twentieth century: the laundry was in the shed beside the house and the family still has some of the equipment. Before 1920 the water came from a well. Mrs Mander's granddaughter Dorothy (Dolly) was born in no. 29 but moved to no. 31 to help her grandmother with the washing. She married Charles Harriss from Yanworth, who was a stone mason. As a sideline he could give you a haircut and a glass of homemade wine for a shilling on a Sunday morning.

Charles and Dolly had three children, Irene, Dennis and Beryl. Irene married Len Vincent and went to live at 2 Wall Farm, where they had a son Brian and a daughter Janice. Len died around 1990. In 1954 Beryl married Ted Ball, who worked for C. J. Howse, first as a bus driver, then as a mechanic maintaining the lorries, and they moved in with her uncle, Harry Mander, at no. 29. Sadly Ted died of a heart attack in 1985. Beryl's uncle Harry died a few years later in 1988. Beryl bought and modernised her cottage and put in a bathroom and new kitchen.

When Mrs Harriss died in 1991 her son Dennis moved to one of the new bungalows in the Approach. For most of his life he has been a gardener, first at Sherborne House, and later for many years for Mr Willes at Ladbarrow. No. 31 Chapel Row, larger than nos. 29 and 30, was converted into an attractive house, with a conservatory where the sheds had been.

No. 30 was for many years home to the Midwinter family, members of which were living in the village in the seventeenth century. Eli Midwinter (1827–1908) and his wife Ann (1829–1901) had two sons, John (1860–1928) and James (1858–1939). Eli worked at Ladbarrow, James at Manor Farm.

Other occupants of Chapel Row at various times from the 1930s were Ken Stevens, Ewart Cook, and the shepherd and the cowman from Blackpits Farm.

New Row, Ashdale Close, Fairfield, The Approach

FOUR pairs of well-built stone houses, nos. 2–9 New Row, were built as estate cottages for the Sherborne Estate in the mid-nineteenth century. They have gardens in front and yards behind, and each has a piece of garden across the road in front. No. 2 used to be occupied by Ernest Sandles, who drove a horsebox and later a lorry for C. J. Howse's haulage firm. He died in 1986, aged 87. His wife Lois used to lay out the dead. She died in 1980, aged 82. Mrs Kathy Smith, who was born Kathy Cook at The Barracks, has lived for a long time at no. 4. Mr Charles Stevens (1898–1971) and his wife Lilian, parents of Ken Stevens, lived at no. 6 after moving from Swyre Farm (where Charles was cowman). The Puffit family now live at nos. 6 and 7. Mr Bob Pitts lives at no. 9, where his mother lived before. Mr and Mrs Dent came to no. 3 in the 1980s. Other occupants of New Row have been members of the Wall, Iles and Howell families.

Ashdale Close was once a haulier's yard belonging to the firm of C. J. Howse. Members of the Howse family were carriers in the village in the mid-nineteenth century. William Thomas Howse (1855–1920) and his wife Elizabeth Ann (1850–1924) lived in Aldsworth in the house now called The Cottage and Mrs Howse ran the Post Office from here from 1888 to 1920. Besides carting goods, W. T. Howse hired out a horse-drawn carriage. The business was continued by his son Basil (1888–1969), who in the 1930s built up a flourishing bus business. Passengers were taken from Aldsworth and the neighbouring villages of The Barringtons, Windrush,

Sherborne and Northleach to and from Cheltenham and
Cirencester. By 1939 there were at least seven buses. The
business continued during the war years. Up to four services
a day were provided on Saturdays and Sundays to
Cheltenham and Cirencester, timed so that people could get
to the cinema and back or go out for a night on the town.
There were then about twelve buses, and at least a dozen
people were employed. Aldsworth residents who were bus
drivers included Ted Fowler, Ted Ball and Ewart Cook (who
married Basil's daughter Joyce). In 1952 Basil sold the bus
business to Marchants of Cheltenham and retired.

Meanwhile Cyril Howse, Basil's son, ran the other side of
the business, which in the early 1930s was mainly coal-
merchanting. Ken Stevens remembers that on Saturdays
when he was not at school he would accompany Ernest
Sandles, one of the drivers. He drove a lorry to Fosse Cross
Railway Station to collect coal, which was then delivered to
households in Aldsworth and Sherborne. Next, three cattle
trucks were acquired. When Ken Stevens returned to the
village in 1946, after serving in the Royal Navy in the Far
East, as a gunner on a defensively equipped merchant ship,
he joined C. J. Howse as a lorry driver, where he remained
for forty-two years. The major part of the business then was
livestock haulage – mainly fat-stock. Cattle would be
collected from the farms and driven to market in Bourton-
on-the-Water, Stow-on-the-Wold, Gloucester, Cirencester,
Lechlade or Kingham. From the market the driver would
usually get another assignment to drive cattle to a
slaughter-house at Ebley near Stroud; Swindon; or Wootton
Bassett – even as far as Islington, London. There were as
many as thirteen lorries and thirteen buses at this time.
Many were parked on the site where the council houses
were later built.

In the 1980s Cyril Howse sold the business to Geoff Harris,
but it continued to trade under the name of C. J. Howse. There
were by now fewer vehicles but these were much larger and
could carry more. In 1988 the firm relocated to a more

convenient site near Witney and the site at Aldsworth was sold for development.

The cottage, office and barn were converted to houses and five new houses were built. The name Ashdale Close was chosen for the area by the developer.

Fairfield, next to Ashdale Close, was built in the 1930s by Basil's brother John, born in 1884.

Three pairs of semi-detached houses, nos. 1–6 The Approach, were built by the local council just after the Second World War. Three bungalows for retired people, nos. 7–9, were built in about 1990.

Longstanding residents at The Approach are Mr and Mrs Stevens (Ken and Jean) at no. 6, Mr and Mrs Crook (Bill and Rose) at no. 4 and Mr Inglis (Sandy) at no. 5.

Cocklebarrow Farm

THERE was a farmhouse and yard at Cocklebarrow in 1799. The fine house, which is there today, dates from the nineteenth century. It stands in a splendidly isolated situation, which is bleak and cold in the winter.

It seems that for some periods of the nineteenth century both the lands to the north of the house, which belonged to Lord Sherborne, and the land to the south of it, which belonged to Christ Church, Oxford (called Rectory Manor Farm and later Manor Farm), were farmed together.

In 1949 the Cocklebarrow Farm land and house were sold by Lord Sherborne to the Hon. E. R. H. Wills. In 1970 the Manor Farm land, about 600 acres, was also sold to Mr Wills. Today the whole is owned by the Hon. E. R. H. Wills of Farmington but leased to and farmed by S. J. Phillips & Sons.

At the time of the enclosure in 1793, William Palphrey was the tenant at Cocklebarrow. He was still there in 1807 with his brother Horatio.

Cocklebarrow Farm House

In the mid-nineteenth century William Jenner Lane, born in 1812, was the tenant. In 1851, aged 38, he farmed 548 acres, in 1861, 909 acres, and in 1871, 1,139 acres. William and his wife Sarah had six children. His son Henry had succeeded him by 1891. By then the Rectory Farm was being farmed by Reginald Slatter.

From 1914 to 1918 the tenant of Cocklebarrow was S. J. Phillips, who lived there with his wife Ruth. Three of their children were born there.

In 1918 Arthur Garne (1890–1963) took over Cocklebarrow. He married Helen Minchin in 1927 and they had one daughter, Joan, born in 1928. She married Oscar Colburn of Crickley Barrow, Northleach in 1951. Arthur Garne kept the tenancy of Cocklebarrow until 1947, but he and his wife continued to live in the house, farming 50 acres.

From 1962 to 1990 Mr and Mrs K. Taylor lived at Cocklebarrow Farm House. Ken Taylor was farm manager for Gregory Phillips, responsible for Blackpits, Cocklebarrow, Woeful Lake and Manor Farm – over 2,000 acres in all.

Ken Taylor first came to Aldsworth in 1953 just after completing his National Service in the Rifle Brigade. Both his parents were vets. From 1953 to 1955 he went to the Royal Agricultural College in Cirencester. One day he explained to his employer, Gregory Phillips, that he had met the girl he wanted to marry but that he had no money for a house, whereupon he was told he would be a far better worker with the right wife and that they could live in the annexe of Blackpits Farmhouse. So Ken and Muriel were married in 1955 and their daughter Jenny was born there. The Phillips themselves had two young children at that time.

From 1956 to 1962 Ken and Muriel lived at Howard's Cottage. Later they swapped houses with Mr and Mrs Arthur Garne, by then in their seventies. They moved to Cocklebarrow and their youngest son, Kennedy, was born there, in the same room in which Gregory Phillips had been born in 1918.

The Taylors remained at Cocklebarrow for twenty-eight years, bringing up their family of four. During this time, one of great prosperity for farming, Ken Taylor took an obvious pride in the efficiency of the business and the smart appearance of the land. If one took a walk from Aldsworth, in any direction and at any time of day, one would be sure to be passed at some point on the way by Ken Taylor in his pick-up keeping an eye on things. He kept an eye on things in the village too: he was a special constable for many years and a parish councillor.

Annexed to Cocklebarrow House is a cottage. On the road to Aldsworth is a pair of semi-detached farm cottages dating from the mid-nineteenth century. At one time they were divided to make four cottages.

Conygree Farm

THE word cony, or coney, means rabbit. Rabbits were not indigenous to England. They were introduced by the Normans and farmed for their meat and fur in warrens. The first recorded mention of Conygree in Aldsworth was in 1571, and it was described as a warren in 1674. 'Conygree Farm' is shown on the 1799 enclosure map on the site of the present farm. To the north of it two fields are called 'West Conygree' (35 acres) and 'East Conygree' (39 acres), and along the road leading to Lodge Park a triangle of ground of about 10 acres is named 'Rabbit Warren' – just where many wild rabbits are hopping about today.

In 1839 Conygree was a farm of 146 acres. Like most of Aldsworth it belonged to Lord Sherborne. The existing house dates from the nineteenth century. William Townsend from Turkdean was manager of Conygree Farm from 1948 until 1967. His daughter Iris married Frank Simpson in 1948.

Conygree Farm has for many years been owned and farmed by Mrs R. Parker, who until recently was a keen huntswoman. She keeps horses for herself and others.

There are two mid-twentieth-century farm cottages at Conygree. One has been occupied for many years by Harry Lockwood.

Lodge Park

LODGE Park lies opposite Conygree Farm. The lodge itself as well as a small strip of land along the road were part of Aldsworth parish until very recently. The 1799 enclosure map shows 'The Lodge' 'part of the Paddock Course', 'Park Plantation' and 'Larcot Hill'.

The Lodge, a unique and beautiful building, was constructed in 1634 for John Dutton of Sherborne House as a 'grandstand' from which to view the coursing of deer by greyhounds. It is now the property of the National Trust.

According to some recollections of Mr Arthur Garne, the beech squares in the park were planted by one of the Dutton family who had been at Waterloo in the same formation as the troops in that famous battle. As the park was designed for Sir John Dutton, Baronet, in the early eighteenth century, it is

more likely to be the battle of Blenheim or another of the
famous victories of John Churchill, First Duke of Marlborough,
that is commemorated here. John 'Crump' Dutton's ghost is
said to haunt Larket Hill.

Lodge Park was the home of the 7th and last Lord
Sherborne and his wife until 1982. In recent years it has been
restored by the National Trust to its original layout as a
banqueting hall and grandstand. It is open to the public and
many fine paintings can be seen there, including portraits of
members of the Dutton family mentioned in this work.

Ladbarrow Farm

L ADBARROW must have been an important site some
2,000–3,000 years ago, when the ancient burial mounds
called barrows were built. A map of 1777 by Isaac Taylor is
marked 'Seven Barrows' near Ladbarrow Farm by the side of
the old racecourse. The area between Aldsworth and
Barrington Downs on the road to Burford is called 'The Seven
Downs'. Near the racecourse 'Three Hedges' is marked and
some distance south 'Square Hedge' – one can only guess at
what prehistoric sites these names can be marking. There is
also the Iron Age earthwork called Dean Camp south-west of
Ladbarrow Farmhouse and evidence of Celtic fields.

Ladbarrow Farm is shown on the map of 1799 in it present
position but the earlier map of 1777 shows no building there.
The house standing there now was built some time in the
nineteenth century. The land beyond it towards Eastleach
where the River Leach runs in a deep valley is quite unspoilt
and very beautiful.

The downs at Ladbarrow were used for horseracing from
the seventeenth century until the mid-nineteenth century, and
probably long before. On the racecourse itself the 'rubbing
house' and the site of the grandstand can still be seen. Much
of the land has never been ploughed.

At the time of the enclosure, Sam Fletcher, a tenant of Lord Sherborne with 703 acres, farmed the land around Ladbarrow.

In 1799 John Garne came to farm at Ladbarrow. Thomas, his son, took over on his father's death in 1823. In 1830 he married Lucy Waine, born in 1794, daughter of Richard and Lucy Waine, but they had no children. Thomas Garne is known to have disapproved of the racing because of the damage done to his crops and stock by the huge crowds. To discourage the use of paths through the fields he used to sprinkle red raddle powder used on rams at tupping time, so that it would mark the ladies' dresses as they passed.

When Thomas Garne died in 1851 the tenancy passed to a nephew, Thomas Houlton (1813–85), whose father had been gamekeeper at Sherborne and whose grandfather had been Lord Sherborne's steward. Thomas Houlton married twice and had twelve children: two sons, Henry and John, by his first wife Bridget Lane, and seven sons and three daughters by his second wife Eleanor Craddock. He was succeeded by his second son, John, born 1848. John married twice. By his first wife, Lucy Waine, he had three children, Florence, Richard Waine and Gertrude. Some time after 1891 George Hewer took over the tenancy of Ladbarrow. The next tenant was Tom Garne, son of W. T. Garne, who took over in 1912. When he died in 1934 his wife and son moved to a smaller farm.

By 1934 Ladbarrow Farm had been sold by Lord Sherborne to Mr Maurice Willes, who came there in that year at the age of nineteen. There were just two sons in the family. The elder, Tom, became a stockbroker with the firm of Roger Mortimer, and it was decided that Maurice, the younger, should be a farmer.

Their father had worked in Argentina, where he met a Dutch baroness who became his wife. They bought Upper Slaughter Manor estate before the First World War. The Willes family came from Cheltenham and had produced many distinguished members of the legal profession since the eighteenth century, including several judges and at least one Lord Chief Justice.

At Ladbarrow, Maurice and his brother Tom kept and trained eight or nine horses – hunters, point-to-pointers and steeplechasers. Maurice was a skilled amateur jockey and rode with considerable success at racecourses nearby – Cheltenham, Pershore, Cole Park, Worcester, Newton Abbott, Torquay, Totnes, etc. His brother was fond of hunting and rode in point-to-points.

Maurice's father died young in 1934 and his mother came to live with him at Ladbarrow. During the Second World War the army moved into Upper Slaughter and after the war the property was sold. Tom Willes, who had given up hunting in favour of shooting, bought a large estate at Corsham. He died in 1999.

In his youth Maurice Willes played tennis, cricket and football. He captained the Aldsworth cricket team and the football team.

Maurice married Valerie Oswald Smith in 1957 and they had one son, Simon, born circa 1958. Mrs Willes, a successful rider at show jumping and other events, devoted her life to hunting, and for sixteen years was Joint Master of the Heythrop Hounds. Her husband and son enjoyed shooting. Mrs Willes died in 1993.

Mr Willes, as he was usually called in the village, supported the church and the village in many ways. For fifty years he was churchwarden, for many years he maintained the churchyard and in 1998 he donated the money to build a tennis court for the village next to the Millennium Village Hall. He lived at Ladbarrow for 66 years, loved his land and made a success of his farming career. Cheerful, good-natured and witty to the end, he died on 13 December 2000, liked and respected by all. He is succeeded by his son Simon.

There are four farm cottages at Ladbarrow; two are near the house and two were built after the Second World War on the road between Ladbarrow and the village. George Edginton came to Ladbarrow when he left school in about 1954 and has been there ever since. His two brothers and his son also work for Mr Willes and live at Ladbarrow with their families.

The Sherborne Arms

THE present-day Sherborne Arms is not the first public house of that name in Aldsworth. An earlier inn called the Sherborne Arms stood at the entrance to the village in 1799. This inn was closed down in 1845 and the schoolteacher's house was built on the site.

As described in Part I of this book, in 1799 there was a house on the site of the present-day pub, possibly the one standing there today. This house, with its gardens and outbuildings on a ¼-acre site, belonged to Richard Waine, born in 1765, the brother of Thomas Waine of Green Farm. It is probable that the Waine family ran a stabling business here from the mid-eighteenth century to the mid-nineteenth century.

Richard Waine married Lucy Meares in 1787 and they had four children, Thomas, John, Joseph and Lucy, all born in Aldsworth. Thomas died at the age of 2. When Richard died in 1821 he left his freehold property to his son John, who in 1841 was described in the census as a stable keeper. By 1831 John had become rich enough to build himself a fine new house – now part of Tayler's Farmhouse.

The second son, Joseph, may have helped with the stables and it is also possible that he was a jockey or trainer in his youth. Nothing is known for certain about his early days, but we do know that in 1833, aged 42, he married Elizabeth Appletree at Hook Norton and that they had nine children. Their first child was born in Chadlington in 1834.

In 1835 Joseph and Elizabeth returned to Aldsworth. We know they lived there for the next ten years because five of their nine children were baptised in the village between 1835 and 1844. Joseph gave his occupation on birth certificates in 1842 and 1844 as a trainer of racehorses. He was described in

The Sherborne Arms

the baptismal records as a training groom and in the 1841
census as a groom. It is not known where the family lived,
but Joseph's brother John had by then built his new house, so
perhaps they lived in the old family home on the site of the
present pub. Joseph may have taken over the racing stables
previously run by William Sadler, which were almost
certainly situated near Aldsworth Manor House. It is
interesting that Joseph returned to Aldsworth in 1835, the
year that racing started up again after a ten-year interval, and
left the village in 1845, the year that racing ended. It is clear
that it was Joseph who ran the racing stables which were
'banished' by the disapproving vicar! Joseph and Elizabeth
moved to Cirencester, where their three youngest children
were born in 1846, 1848 and 1850. Joseph was described in
the 1851 census for Cirencester as a 'victualler'.

By 1861 Joseph and Elizabeth had returned to Aldsworth.
His brother John had died in 1858. John had never married

and probably left his property to his brother Joseph. John's new house was sold to the Tayler family after his death, but there was also the old family home on the main road. In 1861 Joseph was living in Aldsworth with his wife and four youngest children and he was described as a yeoman. His widowed sister, Lucy Garne, was also living with him.

At some time between 1861 and 1871 Joseph's house became an inn, as he is described in the 1871 census as an innkeeper. His daughter Violetta, aged 32, a widow, was keeping house for him and a granddaughter was also living with him. He was then 80 years old. Elizabeth, his wife, had died earlier in the same year and was buried in the churchyard.

Joseph died in 1883 at the age of 91, and was buried in the churchyard next to his wife and sister. His will made in the year of his death mentions his 'freehold property known as the Sherborne Arms Inn'. Thus it was Joseph Waine (1791–1883) who was the first innkeeper of the present pub, the Sherborne Arms.

Joseph also left a farm in Brimpsfield. It and the Sherborne Arms Inn were sold after his death. Taylers Brewery of Northleach bought the Sherborne Arms and in 1891 Charles Collett was the innkeeper. Taylers sold the pub to Garnes Brewery of Burford. It was managed by Mr Crook for thirty years and then by Mr Stocks. The pub was sold in the 1960s to Mr Caudle. He was followed by Mr Briers, Mr Clough and Mr Eldridge. The present owner is Mr John O'Keeffe.

The Sherborne Arms is the ideal country pub. It is very much part of the village but not at its centre, where traffic and noise generated by it might annoy the inhabitants. It is on the main road so it attracts passing traffic, but it is not large enough to cater for coach parties of tourists who would drive away the local customers. It has a garden with a lovely view and a separate room for special events, and for the last ten years it has served excellent food as well as wine.

In about 1990 a new house called Holly Tree House was built next to the pub for Mr and Mrs O'Keeffe's daughter and son-in-law, Mr and Mrs D. Jenvey, and their family.

APPENDIX A

POPULATION

The census figures for the population of Aldsworth in the nineteenth century are given in Table 1. From this it can be seen that the population was 288 in 1801 and rose to a peak of 430 in 1861 before declining to 299 in 1901. It declined still further in the twentieth century to 230 in 1951 and 190 by 1971. It has increased since then, and at the time of writing is just over 200.

Figures for earlier times have to be estimated from the data available. In 1086, with 16 hides (approximately 1,920 acres) under cultivation, twenty-five ploughs and some fifty households, the population was probably slightly larger than today. There were twenty-one households in 1563 and ninety-four communicants in 1603. *Men and Armour for Gloucestershire 1608, by Smyth*, a list of men liable for service with the militia, shows that there were thirty-one men in Aldsworth at that date who had arms and were trained for military service. At a rough guess that implies that there was a population of 250–300 in 1608. There was a low point in 1712. Sir Robert Atkyns, Kt, in his *Ancient and present state of Gloucestershire – 1712* says of Aldsworth, 'There are thirty houses in this parish and about one hundred and twenty inhabitants.'

Table 1: Population of Aldsworth, 1801–1971

Year	1801	1811	1821	1831	1841	1851	1861	1871	1881	1891
Population	288	282	347	353	365	379	430	395	386	372

Year	1901	1911				1951		1971		
Population	299	312				230		190		

Extract from Men and Armour for Gloucestershire, 1608

The Hundred of Brightwellsbarrow
Aldesworth: Wherof the Kings Majestie is Lord

Thomas Cowley yeoman. 1 m
Thomas Meysy. 2 ca ⎫
Samuell Skynner. 2 py. ⎬ servants to the said Thomas Cowley
John Bushe. 1 ca. ⎭
Thomas Brode yeoman. 2 m hath one Corslet fur'
Thomas Brode Jun his sonne 1 ca
Roger Burdocke servant to Thomas Brode sen' 1 p
Thomas Lawrence yeoman 1 p
Edmond Wilkins servant to Thomas Lawrence 1 ca
Thomas Pamor husbandman 3 py
Richard Mauncell his servant 1 ca
Richard Lyfoly husbandman 3 m
Richard Lyfoly Jun' his sonne 1 m
Edmond Cafold servant to Richard Lyfoly sen' 1 ca
John Palmer husbandman 2 ca tr
Will'm Rodborne husbandman 2 ca
Will'm Taylor 2 ca ⎫
Robert Camery 1 m ⎭ servants to the said Will'm Rodborne
James House husbandman 1 p tr
George Taylor 2 py ⎫
Toby Jenkyn ⎭ servants to the said James House
Robert Humfry husbandman 2 p tr
Robert Cowley yeoman 1 p
Lewis Cowley yeoman 1 ca
Lawrence Pullam 2 py
Henry Halle sheppeard 2 ca
Ananyas Rawlings sheppeard 1 ca
Drue Herban Taylor 2 ca
Edward Bernard husbandman 1 ca
Joseph George husbandman 2 ca
Roger Browne laborer

Inhabytants chardged with findinge of Armour not before
mentioned

Thomas Parry unable in body hath one musket and one
Calyver fur'. William Page unable in body hath one Corslet
fur'.

Also the said Tythinge is chardged with the findinge of one
Corslet one musket and ii Calyvers with their fur'.

Probable explanation of abbreviations:
    m = musket
    p   = pike
    py = [not known]
    ca =   calyver

SOME UNUSUAL PLACE NAMES

Blackpits

On the 1799 enclosure map an unnamed house and farmyard is shown on the site of Blackpits House. One mile north-east of the village, a farm-track leading off the Sherborne road to the east is shown, which led to a barn called Black Pit Barn (both barn and farm track are still there today). On the map the track led on to an unenclosed area named Black Pit Downs. Two enclosed fields bordering both the Downs and the track are shown and named North Black Pit Ground and South Black Pit Ground. Sheep were raised on the downs: it is known that pitch was burned to use as a sheep salve in the Middle Ages, and pitch is black. It therefore seems likely that there was a sheep-dip here in early times, probably where the track (now known as Drover's Way) widens out beyond the barn. There was a well here. Blackpits House presumably took its name from the land associated with it.

The Barracks

The name 'The Barracks' given to the house on the lower of the two greens in Aldsworth is unlikely to date from the English Civil War. The word, which comes from the Spanish, originally meant huts or temporary dwellings. It was not in general use in England until the end of the eighteenth century. England did not have a standing army with purpose-built buildings until recent times. In earlier days, troops were raised in time of trouble and billeted on the local population.

There are no written records concerning 'The Barracks' in Aldsworth. The name probably dates from the late eighteenth or early nineteenth century.

In 1793 the French king and queen were executed. France declared war on England and there was a real danger that Britain would be invaded by the French. The local defence forces, called the militia, were called out. Prime Minister William Pitt also called for volunteer troops to be raised.

A troop was raised in Gloucestershire by Mr Powell Snell of Northleach in 1795. In the 1800 Army list this troop is listed in the section 'Gentlemen and Yeomanry Cavalry' as 'Loyal Gloucester', and appears to have been the only troop of this kind in Gloucestershire at that time. There were fourteen officers, a chaplain, an adjutant and a surgeon (see list on page 134). The Hon. John Dutton, who was aged 20 at that time, was a lieutenant. His father, Lord Sherborne, at 56 was probably too old to take part. The ordinary troopers are not named – they would have been 'yeomen': that is, mainly tenant farmers and their sons. Many volunteer forces were raised up and down the land in these years of war with France. The volunteer troops were disbanded after the war.

The year 1830 saw civil unrest in southern England. There were protests against the introduction of threshing machines which threatened labourers' jobs and wages. There were serious riots in Bristol. Troops of Yeomanry Cavalry were formed in Gloucestershire. Although there are no written records, it seems certain that a successor troop to the 'Loyal Gloucester' used 'The Barracks' in Aldsworth as its headquarters. People living in Aldsworth today say that 'The Barracks' was occupied by 'Lord Sherborne's private army'. This must have been how it appeared to villagers at the time. The yeomanry had excellent arms and equipment and a week's training course once a year.

In 1834 the various troops in Gloucestershire were amalgamated into one regiment. Henry Marquis of Worcester (eldest son of the Duke of Beaufort) was appointed lieutenant-colonel of the new regiment; the Hon. James Legge Dutton, aged 30, son and heir of the 2nd Lord Sherborne, was appointed lieutenant-colonel. In 1854 'The Barracks' at Cecily Hill, Cirencester, was built and this became the headquarters of the regiment.

Extract from Army List, 1800

Loyal Gloucester

Major Comm.	Powell Snell	26 Oct 1796
Captain	{ Richard Hippesley	4 Jan 1797
	Humphrey Austen	18 do
	Robert Morris	6 Apr
Lieutenant	{ Thomas Biddle	18 Jan 1797
	Thomas Price	6 Apr
	Hon. John Dutton	19 Apr 1798
	Henry Markham	24 May
	Samuel Jeynes	29 Aug
Second Lieutenant	George Galway Mills	4 Jan 1797
Cornet	{ Henry Hippesley	26 Oct 1796
	George Austen	18 Jan 1797
	Thomas Fuljames	29 Aug 1798
	Thomas Minster	10 Oct 1799
Chaplain	John Neale	21 Dec 1797
Adjutant	James Wintle	29 Aug 1798
Surgeon	Charles Bandon Trye	21 Dec 1797

Agent, Mr Bownas, Parliament Street

Woeful Lake

Woeful Lake Farm lies to the north of Aldsworth in the parish
of Sherborne: next to the house is a 'lake' or large pond.
Several explanations of this extraordinary name have been
given. The most romantic is that it dates from the English
Civil War when a battle was fought here and the lake ran red
with blood. In support of this theory is the fact that Royalist
soldiers came to Sherborne Park after the first battle of
Edgehill and ransacked and set fire to the house, though no
battle is recorded. A sword of the period, said to be that of a
Royalist, was found on Wall Farm land not far from Woeful
Lake in recent times.

On the other hand, some say that the name arises from the
fact that early in the morning on hot summer days, dew

creates a mirage effect and causes a phantom lake to appear in the valley on the left of the house.

A third and more prosaic explanation is that 'Woeful Lake' is a corruption of 'Oldfield Lake'. Bryant's map of Gloucestershire of 1824 is clearly marked 'Oldfield Lake Farm' at this point. The word 'field' on an old map usually indicates an area of land that was cultivated in very early times. There is a tumulus nearby, indicating that there was an early settlement here.

Perhaps all three explanations are true! There is a fourth given by the *Victoria County History*. This attributes the name to the existence of a 'Woe Well', which sounds most implausible.

APPENDIX C

REPORT BY THE REVD JOHN GEORGE BELLINGHAM ON HIS PARISH OF ALDSWORTH, 1859

'Moral condition considerably improved since separation from Turkdean on death of late vicar. Drunkenness was then frequent but is now rare. Races were held in it, training stables supported which attracted a vast crowd of visitors of the lowest and most abandoned description. The public house was thronged on such occasions and pugilistic combats were encouraged and all kinds of games prevailed for the space of a whole week, and caused considerable disorder and licentiousness among the parishioners. But after much persevering effort for above 5 years, the Incumbent succeeded at length in entirely abolishing the races, banishing the stables, suppressing the public house, closing the shops on Sunday, and putting an end to the Sunday games and sports and wrestling, boxing, cockfighting and cricketing which had been usual on the village green. The feeling to the church is highly favourable.'

Biographical details
The following extract is from *Alumni Cantabrigienses* (Cambridge University Press, 1940).

BELLINGHAM, JOHN GEORGE. Adm. Pens. At St John's Apr. 9, 1829 B. in Madras. Matric. Easter, 1829. Migrated to Trinity, Apr. 22, 1831; B.A. 1833; M.A. 1837. Ord. Deacon (London) June 2, 1833; priest, May 25, 1834; C. of Harmondsworth with West Drayton, Middx. 1833–5. C. of St Mary-le-Crypt, Gloucs., 1835–7. C. of Coaley, 1838–9. P.C. of Aldsworth, Gloucs., 1839–65. R. of Begbroke, Oxon., 1869–71. R. of Bagthorpe, Norfolk, 1871–5. R. of Harpley, 1975–86. Disappears from Crockford, 1887. Author, theological.

APPENDIX D

WAR SERVICE

The fallen, 1914–18

Joseph Avery
Joseph Broad
Ernest Broad
Arthur Cook
Norman Fulton
Charles Goodall
John Harris
William Holloway
Edward Hart
John Larner
Thomas Scotford
Albert Tilling
Harry Wingfield

The fallen, 1939–45

Sydney Carter
George Carter
William Paish

Active service, 1939–45

Sonny Aker	Army
George Baxter	Met. Police
Cyril Carter	Army
Reg Carter	Army
Frank Collet	Army
Fred Collet	Army
Jack Collet	Army
Bert Cordrey	Army
Reg Crewe	Army
Bill Crook	Airborne
Ernie Crook	London Fire Service
Alice Cyphus	Wrens

Ted Fowler	Army
Billy Garne	Army
Jack Kite	Royal Navy
Wyn Kite	ATS
Ernie Legg	Army
Fred Mander	RAF
Hubert Mander	Army
Billy Musty	Airborne
Frank Musty	Airborne
Jim Paish	Army
Cyril Palmer	RAF
Gregory Phillips	Army
Fred Pinchin	Army
Frank Robins	Army
Harold Savage	RAF
Jack Scotton	Merchant Navy
Harold Stevens	RAF
Ken Stevens	Royal Navy
Naomi Simpson	ATS
Ernest Vincent	RAF
George Walker	Army
Nora Walker	WRAF
Nigel Wall	Army
Reg Winstone	Army
Dorothy Dickson	ATS
Jim Howe	Army
Harold Harding	Army

National Service, 1945–54

Dennis Harris	Army
Arthur Mander	RAF
John Mander	RAF
Mervyn Sandles	Royal Navy
Gerald Stevens	Army
Sam Vincent	Army

Women's Land Army, 1940–47

Nelly Carter
Maidie Ind
Janet Large
Kath Mander
Nellie Mander
May Parrot
Ciss Pinchin
Lillian Stringer
Nancy Welsh
Vera Welsh

APPENDIX E

SOURCES OF INFORMATION

Past and present inhabitants of Aldsworth and their descendants

Owen Slatter
Ted A'bear
Sue Garne
Phyllis Pike (née Garne)
Richard O. Garne
Maurice C. Willes
Ken Taylor
Ken Stevens
Frank Simpson
Rose Crewe
Beryl Ball
Kathy Smith
David Wilcox
Beryl Wilcox
Anthony Wilcox
Michael Cooper
Zoë Cooper
Molly Bridge (née Houlton)
David M. Waine (descendant of Joseph Waine, 1791–1883)
Beverly Boston (descendant of Thomas Waine, 1792–1842)
Major R. W. Naesmyth of Posso (son of Sara Slatter of
    Manor Farm)

David Waine

David Waine who lives in Cheshire is the great-great-grandson
of Joseph Waine (1791–1883), training groom and innkeeper.
His great-grandfather, Joseph's eighth child, also called
Joseph, moved to Swindon and ultimately to Sheffield.
Unfortunately for David, stories that are usually passed
down the generations in a family did not reach him because
his paternal grandfather died in Sheffield when David's
father was a baby. Wanting to find out about his ancestors,

David has, over the years, assembled a wealth of information from records of baptism and deaths, from marriage certificates and wills, from population censuses and from various other sources. His research has been so thorough and comprehensive that it has enabled him to put together a complete family tree of the Waine family in the area going back to the early 1500s. All this information he has most generously shared. It has been very rewarding to put it together for the first time with other information, such as the inscriptions on the gravestones in the churchyard and the known history of the village, to build up a picture of the Waine family in Aldsworth of whom almost nothing was known before.

Unpublished sources
Parish records
Censuses of population, 1841, 1851, 1861, 1871, 1881, 1891
Christ Church records
1793 Enclosure Act (Gloucestershire County Record Office)
1799 Enclosure Map (© Gloucestershire County Record Office, Reference Number D 1388 Box C)
Jago Cooper, *Graveyard Survey, St Bartholomew Church, Aldsworth* (1990)
John Thurstan Holland, *History Seen from Bibury*
Ruth Phillips, *Short Story of a Farmer*

Published sources
The Victoria History of the County of Gloucestershire (Oxford University Press)
Biglands Collection, edited by Brian Frith (Bristol and Gloucestershire Archaeological Society, 1989–95)
Domesday Book, Gloucestershire, edited and translated by John S. Moore (History from the Sources, general editor John Morris, 1982)
Gordon E. Payne, *Gloucestershire, a Survey* (c. 1940)
A. D. Mills, *Oxford Dictionary of Place Names* (Oxford University Press, 1998)

David Verey and Alan Brooks, *The Buildings of England, Gloucestershire I: The Cotswolds* (Penguin, revised edn 1999)

The Dictionary of National Biography

Kenneth O'Morgan (ed.), *The Oxford Illustrated History of Britain* (Guild Publishing, 1984)

Christopher Hibbert, *The English* (Book Club Associates, 1987)

Iris Origo, *The Merchant of Prato* (Jonathan Cape, 1957)

Joan Johnson, *The Gloucestershire Gentry* (Alan Sutton, 1989)

John Wroughton, *An Unhappy Civil War* (Lansdown Press, 1999)

K. J. Beecham, *The History of Cirencester* (Alan Sutton, 1978)

Mollie Davis, *The History of Winson* (Alan Sutton, 1992)

Sybil Longhurst, Walter Tufnell and Alice Tufnell, *Sherborne, a Cotswold Village* (Alan Sutton, 1992)

Richard O. Garne, *Cotswold Yeomen and Sheep* (Regency Press, 1984)

The Cotswold Sheep (Geerings of Ashford in association with the Cotswold Sheep Society, 1995)

Oscar Colburn, *Farmer's Ordinary* (1989)

W. H. Wyndham Quin, *The Yeomanry Cavalry of Gloucester and Monmouth* (1898)

Jessica Stawell, *Burford and Bibury Racecourses: A History* (Hindsight of Burford, 2000)